# CHASING THE DREAM

# CHASING THE DREAM

## TEN YEARS IN THE UPPER AMAZON

*THE SEQUEL TO DREAM OF A LIFETIME*

**NORMAN WALTERS**

644 Northwest 18th Street
Homestead, Florida 33030
newaltersdesigns@gmail.com

Copyright © 2019 by Norman E. Walters

Book design and production: Columbus Publishing Lab
www.ColumbusPublishingLab.com

Published Internationally by YACUMAMA PRESS. Thank you for buying an authorized printing. By doing so, you are helping to support the publishing and printing industry, which I am supporting by writing this book. I fully support the new direction of e-books, but for me there is nothing like holding a book in my hands and embarking on a wondrous new adventure.

This ditty is a reckoning of specific parts of my life. What you are about to read are true accounts of experiences I have shared with many friends and acquaintances, some named and some not. I have kept everything real, but possibly not in the correct order, or maybe tweaked a bit to offer a better read. Remember: all these details are engraved in the Akashic Records. *Om Tao.*

The purchaser of this book is subject to the conditions that he/she shall in no way resell it, nor any part of it, nor make copies of it to distribute freely, for fear of penalty or prosecution.

LCCN: 2019918074
Paperback ISBN: 978-1-63337-346-4
E-book ISBN: 978-1-63337-348-8

Printed in the United States of America
1 3 5 7 9 10 8 6 4 2

For my mother, Virginia Kate Walters.
She had a dream and never gave up.

For my wife, Carmen, for living through this,

and

for all my children:
Luke
Star
Nayla
Stacy Ann
(as they came into my life).
Forever in my heart,
forever in my soul.

# CONTENTS

| | |
|---|---|
| **AUTHOR'S NOTE** | 9 |
| **PART ONE: TUNCHIS AND GUNS** | 13 |
| Chapter One | 15 |
| Chapter Two | 23 |
| **PART TWO: SURPRISES, SURPRISES, AND MORE SURPRISES** | 29 |
| Chapter Three | 31 |
| **PART THREE: MY SHAMAN, MY HERO** | 47 |
| Chapter Four | 49 |
| **PART FOUR: THE BAPTISM OF THE LODGE** | 57 |
| Chapter Five | 59 |
| **PART FIVE: POACHERS** | 67 |
| Chapter Six | 69 |
| **PART SIX: CALIFORNIA DREAMIN'** | 81 |
| Chapter Seven | 83 |
| **PART SEVEN: HERE COMES DA GROUPS (AND SURPRISES)** | 93 |
| Chapter Eight | 95 |
| Chapter Nine | 106 |
| Chapter Ten | 114 |
| **PART EIGHT: CALIFORNIA AND BEYOND** | 119 |
| Chapter Eleven | 121 |
| Chapter Twelve | 128 |
| **PART NINE: GROUPS, GROUPS, AND THE FISHING MAFIA** | 135 |
| Chapter Thirteen | 137 |
| Chapter Fourteen | 144 |
| **PART TEN: THE TOWER TO THE SKY** | 153 |

Chapter Fifteen — 155
Chapter Sixteen — 166

## PART ELEVEN: A CLOSE CALL — 175
Chapter Seventeen — 177
Chapter Eighteen — 189

## PART TWELVE: POWERS THAT BE — 193
Chapter Nineteen — 195
Chapter Twenty — 202

## PART THIRTEEN: WE'RE ON OUR WAY TO NOWHERE — 211
Chapter Twenty-One — 213
Chapter Twenty-Two — 216
Chapter Twenty-Three — 221

## PART FOURTEEN: BUILDING A LIFE IN PERU — 227
Chapter Twenty-Four — 229

## PART FIFTEEN: HIPPY GOTTA DO WHAT A HIPPY GOTTA DO — 239
Chapter Twenty-Five — 241
Chapter Twenty-Six — 247
Chapter Twenty-Seven — 253

## PART SIXTEEN: THE END OF DAYS — 265
Chapter Twenty-Eight — 267

## PART SEVENTEEN: THE STRUGGLE FOR RECOVERY — 271
Chapter Twenty-Nine — 273
Chapter Thirty — 278

## PART EIGHTEEN: THE CARBON PROJECT — 287
Chapter Thirty-One — 289

## PART NINETEEN: WE MUST SELL THE LODGE — 293
Chapter Thirty-Two — 295

**EPILOGUE** — 299
**ACKNOWLEDGMENTS** — 301
**ABOUT THE AUTHOR** — 303

*Please forgive me for the quality of some of the photographs. This was the Amazon jungle in the 1990s, and negatives and photographs disintegrate with time. I have seen some bad photos in my time, but if you can get a feeling of the moment from them, that is all I can ask for.*

# AUTHOR'S NOTE

**CHASING THE DREAM** is a continuation of *Dream of a Lifetime*, my first book, depicting life experiences I encountered in the Peruvian Amazon rainforest while building the Yacumama Lodge.

The first construction stage spanned one year and nine months, recruiting employees from the closest village of Puerto Miguel, constantly gathering jungle materials (from our land), dealing with the ever-changing "rules of the game," and always trying to stay one step ahead of that game (but when I couldn't I had to clean up the mess).

There were times I felt as though I was facing a hundred-story granite wall with no hand- or footholds. The Amazon rainforest is incredibly beautiful, yes, but it can also be very unforgiving, and if anybody does not observe the "laws of the jungle," they can very easily become a body in the jungle.

Since we were in the middle of the Amazon, 110 miles from the influences of modern-day living, every act, breath, and step had to be thought out and calculated. A mistake could be troublesome, maybe even catastrophic.

The creator of this dream, Lawrence Bishop, and I were building a tourist destination, and in the designing process we had to consider safety, comfort, ease of access, enjoyment, attraction, good food, good service, and most of all…adventure. We agreed upon "rustic, but comfortable."

Some of you reading this book have been to Yacumama Lodge and know what I mean, and others will understand, maybe through osmosis. The story of this dream is very bittersweet, exulting, surprising, and disappointing. So let's get it on! *Ándele*!

*My journey has no beginning*
*My beginning has no end*
*My end has no means*

Norman Walters,
Yarapa, 1993

**NORMAN AND LAWRENCE**
*A SALUTE TO THE GREAT SPIRIT*

PART ONE
# TUNCHIS AND GUNS

*Yacumama Lodge*
*Rio Yarapa*
*Early 1993*

# ONE

**IN THE EARLY DAYS OF 1993** on the *Rio Yarapa* (Yarapa River), 110 miles by speedboat or about seventy-one miles as the heron flies, up the *Rio Amazonas* (Amazon River) from the asphalt jungle metropolis of Iquitos, Peru (one of the largest rainforest jungle cities in the world, that has no roads in and is only accessible from the "outside world" by water or air), I was contemplating the construction progress of our new project: YACUMAMA LODGE.

Now, by *our* I am referring to Lawrence and myself. Partners in adventure for close to fifty years, our newest venture was constructing an ecologically sustainable tourist facility in the middle of the Amazon jungle.

I'm talking deep dark primeval forest, where most of the Native South American *Riberenos* (people who live on the banks of rivers) live in *tambos* (houses consisting of four or more posts set in the clay, a floor of flattened palm tree logs, and a roof of dried palm leaves, most with no walls or divisions) and travel in dugout canoes. **Rustic, baby!**

We had hired ninety-six of the men and women to work with me, building the structural design. What they didn't know I taught them, and what I didn't know they taught me. My partner was the architect, and I was the engineer and builder. His design was sort of Thai, with peaked roofs and eyebrow openings for light and air circulation. These men, for the most part, built only with their machetes.

*The incredible beginning of the main buildings*

*Main buildings, much later. Design completed.*

## CHASING THE DREAM

We supplied hammers, saws, levels, and planes to augment their abilities and speed up the work. The new tools fit right in; everyone was happy. There were a few younger men, graduates of high school, whom I taught how to use the electric equipment. They quickly became my "captains."

Like I was saying, I was contemplating the progress of the construction, sitting in my makeshift office area, when I heard, "*Señor* Norman, Señor Norman...BONES!"

I felt and heard someone running toward me on the wooden *pasadiso* (walkway), and lo and behold, into my office bursts my trusty site supervisor/translator, Esteban. He was talking very fast and appeared to be excited or alarmed.

"They were digging the corner post holes for your house porch, and they uncovered BONES, HUMAN BONES!" he exclaimed. "Come. Come, you must see. They say this is the site of an ancient cemetery."

That definitely brought me out of my reverie. Human bones were not the thing you wanted to find under your house in the Amazon jungle. Wouldn't that be something you'd see in a movie? Wait a minute...breathe.

I tried to calm him down and said, "Show me!"

As we walked down the pasadiso, Esteban relayed what the men were saying:

*Tunchis,* the name they called the ghosts of their ancestors, lurked around burial sites, and because this particular location was probably pre-remembered history, it was hard to tell who they were. The Tunchis could be helpful or destructive depending on what our intentions were. The people of Puerto Miguel (the village closest to us where we procured all the workers) have many verbally documented sightings of Tunchis in their current cemetery across the river from the village. This was new to them.

Okay. Got it! Now I just had to figure out what to do with this new information.

Arriving at the site, I saw nine men standing as still as statues around the freshly dug (in the clay) twelve-inch-diameter hole. Lying on the ground, exposed to the late twentieth century elements, was a broken piece of bone. I knelt down to get a better look, and sure enough it was the knee-joint end of an aged, ochre-colored human femur. This was not the direction I had anticipated us heading, but we were here, and the men were spooked.

I told Esteban, "Return the bone fragment to its rightful resting place (the hole), fill the hole, and I will change the location of the house porch. We will not dig here again."

That seemed to ease some of the fear I had seen in the eyes of the men. I smiled at them, steepled my hands in prayer, turned, walked away, and hoped that they would continue working.

They did, but when I saw Juan (my old "go-to guy") again, I told him about the occurrence, and he had a very strange warning for me. Apparently, when he was younger he had a bad experience with Tunchis in a jungle village. When he recounted his experience, an old man advised him to always sleep with his machete under his pillow. Touching the machete is a show of force and scares the Tunchis away.

From that day forward, I've slept with my machete and my .38 caliber revolver under my pillow while in the jungle.

I was interested in this aspect of the jungle, being interested in the spirit world and having a few unanswered occurrences in my life, only explained through spirit meddling. My mom, sister, and I were transfixed by the Ouija board in the mid-1960s. We were attempting contact with the spirit world and received a bunch of conflicting responses. That didn't stop us, though, and we proceeded until lack of interest set in.

## CHASING THE DREAM

I had been living in my house on the river for some time, concentrating on the construction, when my partner's brother John and his wife Yamuna came to Peru to lend a helping hand. John's carpentry skills and Yamuna's managerial/cooking skills fit in perfectly with our plans.

*Happy guys*

I'll tell you, it was great having someone to converse with in English. I had been on my own, after the initial push with Lawrence in late 1992, for some months. My girlfriend, Carmen (not speaking English yet), and Yamuna got along really well. Carmen's three-year-old daughter, Naylita, was the ice breaker for all of us. So cute. Yes, her pet snake is dead.

*Naylita*

One night while John, Yamuna, and I were sitting around talking, the conversation turned to the *digging up of bones*—you know, a very common topic. They were interested.

Yamuna asked, "Have you had any strange feelings, like heard or seen anything?"

"Well, I have to say that the nights are pretty dead around here, as you have found to be true, I'm sure," I responded.

"No pun intended?" John asked.

"Just kidding, John. It is loud, but silent. If you know what I mean?"

"Yes, the cacophony, when you tune it out, is jungle silence, and it is almost deafening," added Yamuna, smiling.

One regular night, I strolled down the pasadiso to *mi casa* where I typed for a while on my old Royal portable typewriter, logging events in the hope of writing books about my experiences in the Amazon one day.

I did all the things a person does when getting ready to be unconscious for seven hours: changing into jammies, brushing teeth, shooing the mosquitoes away from the bed, dropping and tucking the net in around the mattress, grabbing my book, and climbing into the sleep chamber. I read for a chapter or two in the book *Farm on the River of Emeralds* by Moritz Thomsen (talk about disappointing experiences), turned down the kerosene lamp to a flicker, and surrendered to the inevitable.

Not long after, I heard noises in the silence, almost like ropes being dragged down the pasadiso, and whispered phrases I couldn't make out. I just figured the night watchman was sweeping or something. The noises grew louder, and I decided to raise up to see what the commotion was all about. I was going to push my body up with my right arm. To my surprise, it felt like it was glued to the bed. Actually, I tried to move my *body*, and it was impossible. Now, either some butt-crazy witch doctor had blown curare powder up my nose, or I was dead or dreaming. My mind wasn't sending signals anymore, but my eyes were open, and I was aware of my surroundings. It had to be the curare, and I was Wade Davis in *The Serpent and the Rainbow*.

## CHASING THE DREAM

I struggled, using all of my strength and might, but it was to no avail, for I was paralyzed.

I then noticed that the scraping and murmuring voices were at my door; I could actually see shadows milling around through the screen. The door did not open, but the shadowy figures were appearing inside my room and moving toward the center of the floor.

All of a sudden, the thought entered my mind, *The machete!* Juan had told me to grab the machete. I forced, forced harder, and forced even harder yet. My hand moved, very little, but moved. I looked up and saw the forms starting to encircle my bed, swaying slightly like they were floating. I continued forcing my will into my muscles, and I could feel the actual pressure that I was generating in my body. Holy shit, could I have a coronary or a stroke? I looked up again, and dear Jesus, there were a lot of them. They started brushing the mosquito net as they floated around the bed. Closer and closer, and only one of me, but my hand kept moving, "centimetering" along.

What really bothered me was the murmuring, whispered words not discernable, in no real idiom, and the strange musty smell. It was just plain creepy. I felt the mosquito net begin to stretch inward, and looking out of the corner of my eye at my hand, I saw that I was there.

I grabbed the handle, swung it at the figures (cutting a long slice in the mosquito net), and everything that had been occurring disappeared! Poof, just like that, gone. I looked around, machete in hand, then opened the sliced mosquito net, feeling kind of stupid. I exited the sleep chamber, turned up the lamp, checked the bathroom and every corner. Nothing!

I walked out the door of my house. I hurried down the pasadiso, found our security man, Frank, led him to Esteban's cabin, woke him up, and asked, "Were there any people moving around tonight on the walkway?"

"No, *señor, nadie. Todo estaba en silencio*," responded Frank, looking at me. He added, "*Por qué?*"

Supposedly everything was quiet, but looking at me in a very queer way he had asked me, *Why?*

I asked Esteban to tell him there was no reason. I thought that I had heard something, that was all. "*Buenas noches.*"

"Good night to all," I murmured to myself, walking back to my house. Boy oh boy. Either I was really out of it, dreaming, or Juan was right.

In my gut, I knew the truth: ***TUNCHIS.***

# TWO

**WE REALIZED THAT THERE WERE** far greater dangers in the Amazon than Tunchis, so when Lawrence came the next time we visited our new friend, Rubin. He was one of the brothers/owners of Ari's Burger and a cool guy. He was also known as someone who could get you what you wanted, according to Juan.

We wanted guns!

He had a back room in the restaurant, actually a few back rooms and a large second floor. He led us through a labyrinth of passageways, and as we passed a large open door I was surprised to see a young jaguar chained to a platform in the middle of the room. The cat did not look very happy or healthy. I asked Rubin about it, and he seemed very proud of owning it.

*Hmm.*

We ended up buying a beautiful little Baby Browning .25 semi-automatic pistol; an S&W .38 Police Special chrome-plated six-shot revolver with holster, which became mine; a .410 gauge pump shotgun (we already had a couple .12 gauge single-barrel shotguns); and plenty of ammunition.

## NORMAN WALTERS

We were set—armed and dangerous. I wore that .38 for quite a few years until it was stolen and I had to buy a different one. This next week in the lodge would be fun. We had throwing knives, hatchets, stars, and guns. Now doesn't that sound like fun, girls?

After we worked at the lodge for the week and rocked out at night (he always brought his portable Walkman stereo system) to Led Zeppelin, Def Leppard, old Clapton, Hendrix, and the Rolling Stones, we decided to stay at the lodge for the weekend. Usually we went back to Iquitos every Friday, but he was going to leave for Brazil on the following Friday and wanted to enjoy our jungle home for a while longer. Now we could have some fun.

We always called it "The Gringo Show," because we were *gringos*, number one, but mostly because we were a spectacle. The main building's walls were almost all screen. Put that together with very bright kerosene Aladdin lamps, blasting rock and roll, him and me scurrying around making adornments, and we had an audience every night. We didn't realize it at first, but one night I went out to "leak the lizard" and noticed a wall of canoes in the river and all of our live-in employees on the dock, watching, smoking cigarettes, and laughing their asses off.

Well, we did get a kick out of that too, thinking that what we were doing was interesting. Our cook told Juan that it was better than watching TV. Hey, we displayed new episodes for them every night. We were decorating the lodge, and all the esoteric books we had read gave us a leg up on that. Lawrence loved symbology.

There was a *fútbol* (soccer) game on Sunday in one of the nearby villages, and all the live-in workers wanted to attend and play—I had formed the "Team Yacumama," and we were good. We talked it over and decided that everyone could go, take our speedboat, *Yacuruna,* and have a great time. We would watch the lodge.

## CHASING THE DREAM

They all left around 8:30 in the morning. We relaxed a bit, read, talked, made plans, and walked around looking at the construction. We still had a ways to go, but we were getting there; I believed that we would be ready to have a "Fam Tour" for booking agencies in mid-June 1994. We had half a year to complete it.

"Hey, let's fling some steel," I said, "I want to try out that new hatchet I just bought." We ambled toward the main building, looking for things we could use for targets.

"Grab a couple of those *tablas* (wood boards) to throw at," Lawrence said, "and lean them up against a tree."

"Why, yes sir," I joked. "Just let me take off my pith helmet and put down my riding crop. Cheerio!"

Sidenote: This was in reference to a conversation we'd had over a year and a half before. When explaining to me how easy building this lodge would be, he said that I would be walking around wearing a pith helmet, carrying a crop, and directing the work. I never did get the hat, or the crop, but I did direct the work. I also did a large percentage of the work in the rain, mud, and flood waters.

Now, don't get me wrong, I was not naïve enough to believe what my bubba said, and I am not complaining. All I have ever known is "hands-on" work. You should see my old hands.

Well, he did catch the joke, and we guffawed about it for a bit and then carried on. When we were all set up with tablas for the hatchets, knives, and stars; cans and plastic targets for the guns; and a beer for me (he had his own refreshments); we loaded all the guns, laid out the throwing weapons, and sat back for a moment. It all looked good. Were we ready? Yes, we were ready!

*Gentlemen, start your engines!*

I grabbed my new hatchet, stood back gauging the distance, which seemed to be about twenty feet, and flung my weapon at the tabla. It made a loud noise and bounced off. Just a little more of a revolution and the second one stuck deep into the wood.

I looked over; he was flinging his hatchet too, and his knife was on the ground. His hatchet stuck on the first throw. I threw my knife and it stuck. The stars were easy; they have points all the way around the circular base.

We went about our play for a while and agreed that we were ready for the real artillery. There was an old dead tree twenty-five feet away, and I figured we could use it to sight in the guns. Him with the Browning .25 and me with the .38, we started blasting away. After each six-slug round we looked closely at the tree. You could see where my .38s went, and it was not the best formation (a fixed barrel sight). Unfortunately, the .25 slug is just a bit larger than a .22, and we couldn't see the holes in the tree. I thought I discovered one, but a worm crawled out of it as I watched.

"Okay, you shoot, and I'll watch," I said.

Blam…blam…blam…blam…blam…blam, and I just didn't see a single disturbance on the surface of that tree. I walked up to the tree and studied the surface. Nothing. That 2.11-inch barrel is not for long distances. It is for very close bodily contact. He moved up about fifteen feet, and on the next round all six hit the tree. Voila. The thing was, I couldn't shoot at the tree with him in front of me, so I picked a different target. We banged away for a while, then switched to shotguns and really had fun blowing targets to pieces. In about an hour we'd finished off all the ammunition and had to go back to our caveman instincts, throwing sharp objects at the tablas.

Without the deafening blasts I started to hear noises behind us and swung around with my hatchet in my hand. A small audience had gathered. Some of our workers from the village had paddled up to the lodge. One of the younger ones spoke very broken English, and he tried to tell me that they heard the guns and feared for our lives since all of our live-in employees were gone. They thought we were being attacked by the *terroristas!*

As I have said before, there are no secrets in the jungle. We had definitely lost our macho man attitude. I tried to stumble through apologies and smiles, thanking them for their concern.

We surveyed the mess we had made, then started cleaning it up. At least everyone would know we were armed. Then Lawrence had a great idea.

"It's still early; let's go fishing," he urged.

I hadn't noticed, but two of our live-in employees were in the group of villagers. Through hand language I told them that we were going fishing, and they could watch the lodge. We grabbed our gear, hopped in the wooden boat with the twenty-five-horsepower motor, and off we went.

One of the many diversions that we enjoyed immensely was fishing. We would motor up the Cumaceba Creek to one of the lakes and fish for hours. It was just like a *National Geographic* magazine come to life. The birds were the most interesting attraction. Huge tiger, blue, and white herons would swoop down, actually trying to get our fish while we were reeling them in. What a spectacle.

While we were lazing in the wooden boat, feeling laid back and groovy, he grabbed his pole and exclaimed, "I got a big one." He reeled and reeled and pulled and pulled, and there was more and more resistance.

We both thought he had the big one. The mother of all fish. He kept reeling it in, little by little, until it was close to the boat. Up it came, and when it broke the surface our jaws dropped. It was an army combat boot. In the middle of the remote Amazon jungle? I have always wondered about that.

Another time, when Carmen and Adriana were fishing with us, we had caught a few good-sized piranhas and an eighteen-inch mota catfish, enough for a good lunch. All of a sudden Lawrence came alive. He had something on his line. He fought it around and around the boat, and when he finally pulled it in we were amazed. It was an eighteen-inch arowana.

You know about fish stories, measurements, and general lying? Well, within a year that fish had grown to thirty inches long and was the record arowana catch of all time. That is one of the things I love about fish stories and urban legends.

## PART 2
# SURPRISES, SURPRISES, AND MORE SURPRISES

*Yacumama S.R. ltd.*
*1993-1994*

# THREE

**YOU KNOW, I DIDN'T REALLY THINK** all that much about the legality of what we were doing in the first year of our construction. My partner had told me that he had purchased 50,000 hectares from Manuel through his new friend the Dolphin Lady, whom I will refer to as DL in the future. He had met her through another friend, and she had invited him to the Earth Summit '92 in Rio de Janeiro.

After the summit and visit to her installation for the care and re-introduction of wounded dolphins in Brazil, he had come to Iquitos, Peru, to see the parcel of land and a lodge that she was representing to sell for quite a bit more than spare change. He told me that there had been a translator (because he spoke little Spanish) to read the document and explain the details. He seemed to be satisfied, and said he had title for the land. I was still deciding whether to be a part of this or not, so for me it really didn't matter. In those early days I still viewed the project as "his baby." I was just building it and helping to support it.

Until…I decided to go forward, partner up, and live my life in Peru for some unforeseen period of time. Then I asked to see the document, which was in Spanish. I didn't read Spanish all that well yet, either, but I did notice that the name of the old lodge was repeated over and over in the script. That seemed kind of strange. It had been printed on a computer, and sort of looked like a simple bill of sale to me.

I asked Juan how I could find the deed and title for the land, and he told me, "We have to go to the *Registro Publico* (district registrar's office), and they will look it up."

Easy enough to do, right? Then I could get a copy and have one of the most important documents a company could ever have: title for the land that we were building on and had already invested over $100,000 in.

Juan and I took the one-page document to the registrar's office, got our ticket, and stood in line to wait our turn. I'd learned by that time that Juan knew someone in every office and agency in Iquitos. I saw him catch the eye of one of the agents and make a hand sign to the man. Now, this was a very important gesture, not to be forgotten.

The thumb and the index fingers were held up, with about a quarter of an inch space between the two finger pads. Come to find out that is the same as saying, "Can I ask you something?" I'd remember that.

The guy nodded, and Juan walked over to talk to him. There were about eight people in front of me. Juan looked over, beckoning me to come. I self-consciously ambled over, and Juan asked me for the paper. I handed it to him, and he handed it to the man. Juan said something in Spanish, and the man said a very long something back in Spanish.

Juan looked at the man and thanked him, turned to me and said, "Let's go!"

When we got outside the office, Juan looked at me with concern and said, "This document has never been registered, and it is just a *compra/venta*, a bill of sale, for the *name* of Manuel's old lodge. He is a squatter, there illegally, and it says very clearly that you are buying 'only the name.' No land. We should talk to a lawyer."

## CHASING THE DREAM

Lawrence was not in Peru, so I called him in Hawaii where he was living. I relayed the story, and he really had nothing to say except, "No way...are you sure?"

I told him that I was going to talk to a lawyer and call him back with the results. Juan said that he knew a lawyer to talk to, and his office was just a few blocks away. The short of it was: We would have to incorporate and apply for a land concession or just keep going on as we had been and pray for the best (that lawyer was not the one we chose to represent us).

This was something to really think about. I called the DL, asked about the document, and inquired for the title. She hesitated a bit too long before answering that she would look into it.

The next weekend I called again, and was informed that it was unfortunate, but the document was what Lawrence had signed for and bought: "The Amazon Lodge." Okay, I had the history lesson, and we had the true story. Lawrence had to come to Iquitos.

In Peru, they call a lawyer or *abogado* "Doctor," so we were going to visit Dr. Teddy T. We walked to his office, rang the doorbell, and the receptionist came to the door. I guess she recognized Juan, because she opened the door wide and asked us to take a seat.

About five minutes later she asked us to follow her. I saw Juan checking out her curvaceous posterior, which was swinging back and forth like a barn door in the wind. Dr. Teddy looked the part, with his black framed glasses, oiled hair, and pencil mustache.

I guessed that Juan's father had been a bureaucrat in the system and knew everyone; hence everyone knew Juan as soon as he mentioned his last name. It was kind of cool to see and be a part of. I guess that we knew when we first met Juan, a scoundrel for sure, that he was just the go-to guy that we needed for situations like this (believe me, this was just the beginning).

I gave Dr. Teddy T. the document, and he read it. He basically told Lawrence, who had just arrived from the USA, that he could use it for toilet paper. It had no use whatsoever because we were not using the name of Manuel's old lodge, which was not even registered or copyrighted.

"What can we do?"

Dr. Teddy T. looked at us and inquired, "Do you have money?"

Hesitantly, Lawrence replied, "Yes...but why?" Like we didn't know, waiting for the other shoe to drop.

Then he surprised us. "Because the president has made a temporary option giving foreigners a chance to buy land in the government-owned areas." He told us that we would have to try to buy it again in the same place. Would that even be possible?

He said that he would help us, and that he could also create a corporation for us. We were opening a business, so we would need to become legal. At that time, 1993, you also needed a Peruvian partner to own a business, and he would be our partner. It could work so easily.

First off, we needed to obtain property rights and not lose everything that we had built in the last year. Dr. Teddy T. gave Juan a name in the *Ministerio de Agricultura* (Department of Agriculture), which we will just call the "Ag office" from here on out, and off we went after thanking him profusely.

I wanted to catch them before they closed down for *siesta*. Every day at around noon, the businesses, banks, government agencies, and the actual people too close down for three to four hours. They come back at 3:30 or 4:00 in the afternoon and work until 6:30 or 7:00 in the evening.

You can probably guess how things worked in the evening. Have you ever worked for three and a half hours, gone home to eat and sleep for a few hours, and then gone back to work for another three and a half hours? Try it and see how alert you are at about 4:30 p.m.

## CHASING THE DREAM

We trudged up the stairs to the Ag office. Juan introduced us to the receptionist, saying that we needed to speak to the head of the department. She asked us to take a seat, and she sashayed down the hall. It seemed that all the receptionists were contortionists. She came back shortly and ushered us into a large office down the same hallway.

When we entered there was no one in the office; it sort of looked abandoned. We only waited three to four minutes, and in walked a man with rolled-up shirtsleeves and a determined look on his face. This had to be the boss. Juan explained the situation and tried to explain where the land was. The boss man pulled out a large quantity of rolled-up maps, laid them on the table, and started searching for the area that Juan had described.

The map that he chose was definitely the Yarapa area. I studied it for future reference as he asked us to point out the area in question. Since there were hardly any notations on these maps, I tried to picture in my mind the twists and turns of the Rio Yarapa where our construction was located. I placed my finger on the largest bend of the river, after the village of Puerto Miguel, which was the only *pueblo* near us. This bend in the river was where our camp was, right after the confluence of the Cumaceba Creek and the Yarapa River. Lawrence and I agreed: we nailed it.

The boss man, Señor Padilla, looked at the area very closely, went to his desk to retrieve a magnifying glass, and studied the surrounding topography. After a few minutes he looked at us and said with a smile, "*Es possible. Esta area estaria disponible para la compra.*" Juan translated, "It is possible. This area would be available for purchase." The land was all owned by the government.

Hey, I liked this guy. The first really positive response of the day. I stumbled through asking how we would go about buying it. He looked at Juan with a questioning expression. Juan cleaned up my train wreck. I guess I wasn't ready to communicate in Spanish yet, but I had tried.

He explained the process, and Juan translated. It was kind of simple, really, and we could do it without many problems. Great! (I still hadn't learned that you never took anyone for their word in the jungle.) We scheduled a meeting with the agriculture engineers for the following day. No time to waste.

● ● ●

When Lawrence had heard the first bad news about the fraudulent deal, he really couldn't believe that his "friend" would do something like that.

I said, "Well, buddy, maybe she isn't your friend!"

"I can't really believe that," he argued. "We had such a good time at the Earth Summit in Brazil, and we were so connected, believing that we could make a difference in the world. I owe her."

"Uh-huh," I said, "I know, but you remember that I've never trusted her motives. I've told you that every time I've delivered your monthly donation to her."

"Well, I still don't believe that she could have known that there was no title or land."

"You could be right. She's only been on the Yarapa, a neighbor of Manuel, for fifteen years. How could she know?" We differed on that point, but there was no reason to beat a dead horse.

● ● ●

Sr. Padilla, Sr. Rimachi, and two other gentlemen met us in the Ag office, offered us their hands, and then offered us Inca Cola (the famous phosphorescent-yellow Peruvian soft drink, which tastes like bubblegum). Juan was with us to translate. They already had their maps

# CHASING THE DREAM

stretched out on the table, and I had done some investigation as to the real location of our construction.

As we studied the map, it was easy to see where we were located. The Dolphin Lady's lodge (that we were using as base camp one while we built the first phase of our project) was located at the confluence of the Yarapa River and the Cumaceba Creek, so I knew exactly where I was looking. I just followed the river upstream until I reached the bend that we called home.

Sr. Rimachi, the main forest engineer, marked the DL's lodge (squatting also) and our future Yacumama Lodge on the map. Lawrence decided that it was the right time to explain what he desired to achieve with this project. Juan was the type of translator who could listen and translate all at the same time, so when my partner and I were talking he was translating. Really something to behold.

"We are interested in trying to protect as much of this area as permitted from poachers and loggers. There is a village named Puerto Miguel close to our project, and they rely on the surrounding jungle to maintain their families and their village. When outside poachers come into the area to cut down trees and kill animals for their own commercial gain, it hurts everyone in the village. We want to work with the village, which is 110 miles by river from Iquitos and the nearest real civilization, to protect and preserve the area, helping them ensure a future for their children and their children's children," and so forth and so on.

All four of them looked at him like he had a third or maybe even a fourth eye, but he continued on. "That is why we are trying to secure both sides of the river for a good distance: to create a buffer zone that we can control somewhat. Everyone has to travel past our lodge because there is only one entrance into the Rio Yarapa. I know that we can't stop poaching or logging, and I know that some of the villagers are poachers and loggers, but if we can offer jobs and medical and educational assistance, we may be able to turn the tides just a bit."

I guess it was just weird, or Lawrence had grown a third arm, because no one said a word for about thirty seconds, staring at us. Then they all woke up, looked at each other, and started talking all at once. The first thing I was able to make out was something about *el projecto*, then *el pueblo*, and then *mucho dinero* (the project, the village, and a lot of money).

I believe that he might have gotten through to them a little bit. Please remember, these guys went to college to learn about the jungle land, what makes it up, and how to manage it to keep it healthy. They should have been on our side, with similar beliefs, and they just might have been. It was hard to say at that point.

Whatever the case may be, I had the feeling that they were going to help. There was a different feeling in the air. The "force" had a smooth, free-flowing consistency: the "ripple" was gone.

We worked for an hour or more, Lawrence pointing out what we wanted and the engineers checking boundaries, making notations on their legal pads. In the end it appeared as though we had a real "reserve" started here. We could try to preserve a small portion of the Amazon rainforest. Now the rubber would hit the road!

● ● ●

It was time to get started with the busy work. The three of us went back to Dr. T.'s office and related the whole meeting, and he was smiling.

Our world brightened again. I guess life is kind of like the rotation of the Earth in relationship to the Sun: light/dark… light/dark…light/dark. We completed the corporation papers with Dr. Teddy, attempted to draw up a timeline, enjoyed each other's company for a few days, and then went our separate ways, doing what we do the best.

## CHASING THE DREAM

The next months were filled with building difficulties, land and title details, coordinating meetings for surveys, boundaries, and living the life.

Sr. Padilla suggested that they visit the lodge to better understand the project and see it first hand for themselves. Now, there was a guy who thought. We made plans for them to visit the coming week on Wednesday. They were taking their speedboat, knowing it was a long trip, and I didn't even have to give them gas. I told them to come around midday and have lunch with us. It was a date with four hairy guys…lovely.

Wednesday came around, the clock was creeping up to midday, and I was at the lodge trying to pull everything together. We'd eat lunch: grilled doncella fish steaks, Russian salad (steamed cubed beets, potatoes, and carrots, with an eggless mayonnaise dressing), rice, local beans, *chifles* (thin sliced green cooking bananas fried in sunflower oil), and a fresh fruit drink of camu camu (pink in color, now in season).

After lunch we'd take a quick ride up the Rio Yarapa to see the lay of the land, then come back to the lodge to go over the maps.

The conversation at the lunch table was mainly explanations and statements concerning our projected plans. I believe that we were beginning to get through to them, and they were thinking of us as investors in Peru rather than crackpots. I think the change started happening when they saw the design and construction of the main building. We were eating lunch in that building and it was impressive, if I do say so myself!

The Thai-style roofs and the eyebrow openings were not a common design and took skill to design, construction knowledge, and the ability to execute. The high ceilings inside the main lodge and the overlapping roof structure allowed superior ventilation; the lodge always felt fresh and airy.

Lunch afforded more opportunity to explain the problems that we were facing. Lawrence had been fraudulently led to believe that he was buying 50,000 hectares (123,552.5 acres) for $35,000, which was quite a deal. He believed that we could create a "no-fly zone" for

*Yacumama Lodge*

flora and fauna from poachers and the ravages of depredation (this was 1993, and INRENA, the ecological agency in Peru, was still in the womb).

It appeared to me that they were starting to understand what he had been talking about. After lunch we piled into the boat and began our jaunt upriver. The Yarapa area is a very beautiful realm, with overhanging trees 150 to 200 feet tall and black water (clear, but tea-like) with a smooth, mirrored surface. It was deemed an incredible natural zoological kingdom.

The engineers were very impressed; not one of the four had ever been to the area. I could see thoughts and ideas starting to form behind their eyes, and I really wanted to believe that it was not just the money that they could skim. Forgive me, but I was already beginning to understand how the system worked in the jungle. It is called *"coima"*—bribery, money under the table, payola, whatever you want to call it—but it *ruled* in the realm where we were creating our dream.

Natural beauty may be able to conquer some of the nasty underbelly operations of the world, though, and I believe that these men were being touched by its magic wand. I was and still am touched. Every time we pulled into the mouth of the Rio Yarapa from Iquitos, I could feel the magical tranquility.

When we returned from the cruise, the engineers wanted to have a private powwow before we started perusing the maps. They stayed in the boat while we returned to the main lodge. Fifteen minutes later they appeared, maps under arms, ready to get down to it. I guess the results

## CHASING THE DREAM

*The peaceful Rio Yarapa*

of the powwow were positive because they rolled out the map, started looking at border lines, and made small notations here and there.

They talked amongst themselves, uttering yesses, nos, and hmms. Sr. Padilla began: "You are starting a business, and you can purchase land around your construction area. You can also purchase the large conservation area you indicated. There are already areas of named government land that we can cut into. It looks like for the business you will be able to purchase around 400 hectares. These are not encumbered by any other possession rights and are free and clear. One of the boundaries on the south side is a creek. This makes it easier.

"The personal parcel is different. As we were looking at the map we noticed that, from the creek that borders the business's southern limit, there is space enough to sell you the hectares available, with many kilometers of river frontage that connect to your business property, like Sr. Lawrence indicated at our meeting."

# NORMAN WALTERS

*Sr. Padilla and the guys from the Ag office*

Lawrence had projected boundary lines on their maps the day of our meeting in their office. These were similar.

They conferred, and all nodded in affirmation. They studied the map again, appearing to be looking at the other side of the river. A bunch of pointing, hmmming, and raised eyebrows later, it appeared to me that they had reached an agreement.

Sr. Padilla said, "It is our conclusion now that we can sell you river frontage on the other side also. We do understand what you are trying to do, and we would like to help."

The size of the property was not as large as Lawrence had wanted, but it equaled around 3,000 hectares. By the looks of the map we could actually have had an incredible amount of river frontage and been able to monitor some river passage. Those three parcels would have added up to 3,400 hectares, or 8,400 acres. A far

## CHASING THE DREAM

cry from 123,500 acres, but hey, we were basically having a reality check now, if you know what I mean.

With this transaction we could pull ourselves out of the hole, own and protect the land, and go on building the rest of the facility. Sounded like a winner to me. They packed it up, we made a date for the next week to work out the particulars, and I went back to building a jungle resort.

To make the long and the short of it "short" (it went on and on for me), I will call the cows home and finish it. I trudged through the Peruvian bureaucracy and inched toward our goal.

Lawrence decided that since the DL was our neighbor we should not keep all 400 hectares for ourselves but split it up between our two organizations. This was a surprise for me, but since she actually owned nothing on the Yarapa, a squatter herself, he wanted to help her.

Great. I set it up with the Ag office to make two deeds for the small business parcel, 200 hectares each. The DL signed for hers and received the title. The business parcel passed, I signed the title (me being named general manager, partner, and legal representative), and the land went into the Yacumama S.R.Ltda. Corporation. We were on our way. We had land, a business corporation, a Peruvian partner, and money in the bank. We were stylin'…weren't we?

The large parcel took longer to process, and when they were ready to write up they realized that Lawrence couldn't have all 3,000 hectares titled in his name—there was a 1,500-hectare limit. It had to be broken into two parcels, one on each side of the river. He asked the DL to temporarily hold one parcel in her name until the law changed and he could own both.

I only made one comment concerning that decision: "Oh really? Do you think that is prudent?" (It really doesn't matter now if it was or wasn't.)

When the law finally changed fifteen years later she said, "What? That is my land. It is in my name. I'll sell it to you!"

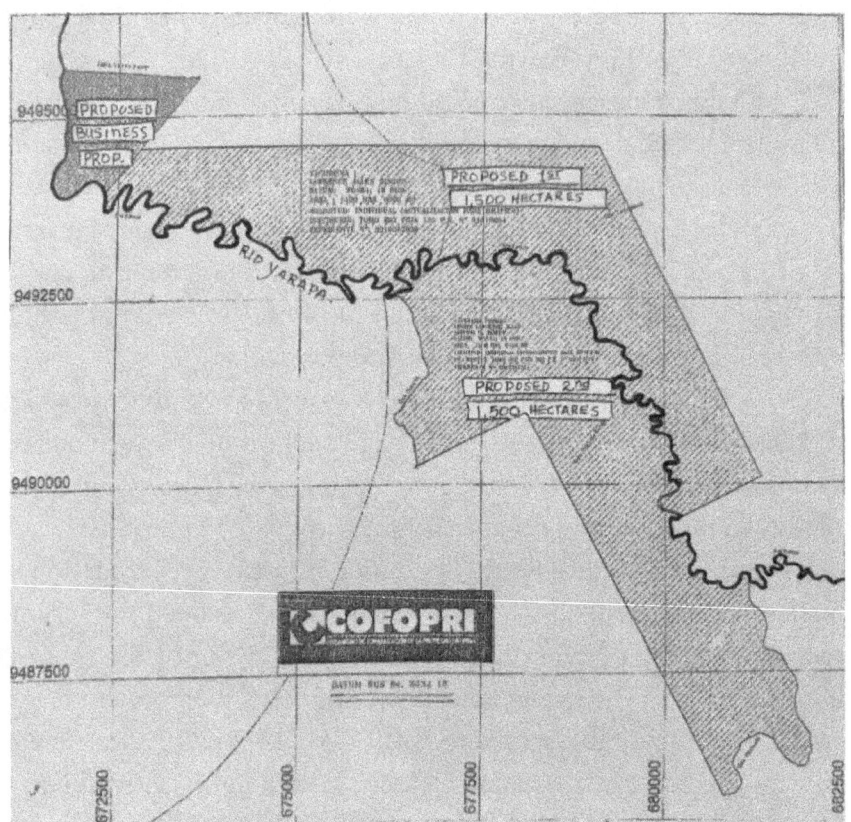

*Business property, first and second parcels*

(He bought it back from her for twenty times the price I paid originally. Titled to him and his wife.)

I had the Ag office guys prepare the titles, paid the price (literally), and that was the real wet kiss. LOL. Hey, what can a body do? I was going to continue with what I was doing: building a tourist resort.

●●●

## CHASING THE DREAM

As soon as all the paperwork was taken care of, the rubber had to meet the road: surveying and boundary lines. I am talking kilometers and kilometers, miles and miles of boundary lines to strike, measure, and mark. The rain was beginning, and the rivers were rising. That's right, it was flood time again. But this year, 1994, was the year of years. The river would rise eighteen inches above all recorded marks on trees (luckily, I had built the lodge one meter—over thirty-nine inches—above the highest mark ever), and the jungle would be all water, river to river to river, no land!

Yacumama Lodge looked like a floating city, especially beautiful at night, with the flames from the oil lamps reflecting off the water around the walkways. That is an indelible sight, unable to be erased with time.

I hired two *topografos*—surveyors—who worked with the Department of Agriculture to come to the lodge and measure and mark all of the boundaries for the properties. I hired an extra crew from the village to work with the topografos in the jungle. We cast twenty-five six-foot-tall concrete corner post markers. For the first month they were able to go into the jungle for a week at a time, camping and preparing their meals with one of our cooks, and me replenishing the food stock every few days. Then the water reached the land and they were in canoes, up to their waists in water all day every day, and returning at night to sleep at the lodge since there was no land left to camp on.

This went on for two more months. When it was finished, I threw a party. We celebrated the end of hemorrhaging money, time, and energy. Hip, hip, hooray!

We went back to our normal construction regimen, and the topografos went back to Iquitos, rich men, to draw the maps. All the details were wrapped up, and I received the registered land titles and maps in April.

This chapter of my epic adventure was over, and I bade it farewell with a beer and my magical black cigarette at Ari's Burger.

## PART 3
# MY SHAMAN, MY HERO
*Lambayeque, Peru*
*1993*

# FOUR

**THE OLD MAN CROUCHED** by the edge of the blazing campfire, his grey hair like steel in the firelight. He wasn't a big man, but his presence dominated the ambience. We sat, waiting in anticipation for the ceremony to begin.

While we waited, I thought about how this whole predicament began: When I first arrived in Iquitos, Peru, in late 1992, I dated the receptionist from the hotel where I was staying. She was a cute girl, bubbly and fun (for a while). After Lawrence returned to the U.S. and I was left in a strange new world to build our new project, a tourist lodge deep in the jungle, it was nice to have someone waiting for me when I arrived back in the city every Friday afternoon.

I only passed the weekends in the city, returning by speedboat every Sunday afternoon to our jungle construction site. This relationship was copacetic (of course I had my own house by that time), and continued for a couple of months until I began feeling the presence of possessive claws in my psyche.

It was a gradual thing, and I tried to work around it. It got worse and worse until the relationship wasn't fun anymore. She was playing mental games with me to see how much controlling power she possessed.

The beginning of the last straw was her breaking off a date, saying that she didn't feel well and couldn't come to my house. At 2:00 in the morning, she called and woke me up, saying that she wanted to come over now she was free.

I let it happen twice over the following weeks, and on the third serving of shit I said, "No, don't come over."

She called two more times that night, crying, at 3:00 and 4:00 a.m. I told her I didn't want to see her anymore and broke off the relationship. It was over for me, *but not for her.*

In the preceding couple of weeks, when we were still kind of together, she had invited me to dinner at her parents' house. Okay, different kind of food, but I was walking on the wild side anyway. So sure, I went. A very weird scene occurred where she acted like a ten-year-old, though she was in her mid-twenties.

What was explained to me later, when the effects of that dinner began to show, was that her mother was into the local witchcraft and had put a special powder in my food. Not a nice powder but a very bad powder, to be exact. That bad powder would control my libido to the extent that I could only be aroused sexually with her daughter, and guess what? It worked, except I never went back to her again. I just couldn't get aroused with anyone else either. The night I told her it was over was the night it was over, literally.

Of course, you guessed it: the calls in the middle of the night didn't stop. Luckily I was only in Iquitos for two nights a week, and I just stopped answering the phone at night. Finally, at long last they stopped, but the effects of the evil powder didn't.

## CHASING THE DREAM

• • •

I met my next girlfriend, Carmen (later to become my wife), in March of 1993 at Ari's Burger, my favorite restaurant in Iquitos. We went dancing a lot and ate out at all the local restaurants. I cooked in my house sometimes (mostly breakfast), but more often we ate out. When we began getting serious, I had to fess up and tell her that I had a problem and that it had nothing to do with her. Carmen was very attractive, petite, and loving.

We had gotten hot and heavy a couple of times (you know, kissing and caressing certain parts of the body) in the first three or four months, but at a certain point I just had to say, "Sorry." That did not boost my self-confidence very much, but hey, what was I to do? What can you do with a limp hotdog?

When we really wanted to start an intimate relationship (I remember it being around May or June) she told me that her brother-in-law's father was a shaman, *curandero*, *brujo*, witchdoctor (whatever you want to call them), and could probably help break the black magic spell cast over me. He only worked in *magica blanca*, white magic.

Things couldn't get any worse, could they? I figured that I'd give it a try. He lived in a village to the northwest, over the Andes Mountains, called Lambayeque. We flew on the now-defunct Faucet Airlines to Truhillo, then on to Chiclayo, and finally by car to the village of Lambayeque.

It was late afternoon by the time we arrived at Don Alejandro's house. Carmen had been in contact with him prior to our trip, and he meditated on my problem in anticipation of our visit. We greeted him and his wife, and he motioned us into a back room. There he explained that this spell was a very strong one, and that a person without the inner strength that I possessed probably would have gone *loco*.

He told me with a thin smile, "*No te preocupes, usare todo mi poder para romper esta mala magia.*" He would use all his power to break the bad magic.

I needed all the help I could get. I wanted to get back on the fast track and live like a normal person…yes ma'am!

So there we were, sitting on a stone bench waiting while Don Alejandro cooked up some San Pedro cactus juice for us to drink. Carmen didn't speak much English yet, but I was well on my way to having a working knowledge of the Spanish language. I could catch the drift of the conversations.

His altar was incredible. In the center of the *huerta*, or outdoor patio, he had ceramic statues of the saints (San Pedro was the largest, but Maria was there with the baby Jesus in her arms), a lot of lit candles, two medium-length swords stuck in the earth (I wondered about those), smoking incense, some sort of shields, and a cloak. It was the first time I had witnessed a ceremony like this, so I was kind of awestruck, being from Indiana and all.

I mean, before this happened to me magic was a tricky thing; some people used it for satanic rites. I guess that could be deemed the same type of magic that had been used on me: make me pay and suffer. That is pretty sick.

I remembered my trip through Manaus, Brazil, to Iquitos. Blood, flowers, severed animal heads, and dead chickens along the road to the airport. The taxi driver called it Santería offerings, not to be confused with voodoo. The two stem from different roots: Spanish Catholic and French Catholic respectively.

Back to the story.

Darkness had fallen, engulfing us in a very dense atmosphere. The huertas in Peruvian houses were open to the elements, and I looked up to see the full moon staring at me through wispy grey clouds. The darkness

## CHASING THE DREAM

*Norman and Don Alejandro in Lambayeque, Peru*

was a little oppressive and felt like a cloak on my shoulders.

I looked over at Carmen, and the candle glow was reflecting off of the topographical planes of her face. She looked at me and smiled. Man, she was beautiful, and I felt good.

Don Alejandro finished stirring the brew and decanted it on his altar. He looked at us and asked a few questions. Yes, everything was good, and yes, we were relaxed and trusting in him. He was crouched in front of us peering, like into our souls, and I perceived a vast, open space behind his eyes. They looked like they had no irises, just big black pupils. Sort of like those Keane paintings.

He stood up, turned, walked to the altar, and felt the bottle of cactus brewsky. I guessed that it was reaching drinking temperature, because he poured it into two small earthen cups, turned back to us, and offered one to Carmen and one to me.

Oh boy, I knew of this stuff. A lot like peyote, I was sure, dark green and as bitter as gall. It wasn't a problem for me; I had taken many an herb in my life for purification of the body and soul, but Carmen hadn't, and anything that was a tiny bit green and bitter made her retch. So she only swallowed a little of the first sip, spit out the rest, and didn't want any more, no matter how Don Alejandro or I coaxed her. Of course I drank mine and a bit more for good measure.

# NORMAN WALTERS

It was almost 2:00 in the morning by the time everything started taking shape. Don Alejandro had been quietly chanting while we waited for the San Pedro to seep into our consciousness. As he chanted into the night sky, he would pick up a thin bottle of an aromatic liquid (Florida water), take some into his mouth, and aspirate it over the fire and into the sky.

All of our surroundings were becoming more defined, colorful, and connected somehow. My thoughts started turning into faint visions (I guess you could call them hallucinations, maybe), and there was a kind of cellular tracing when I moved my eyes from location to location; hence the connection.

I believe that the Don, by his chanting and aspirating, was balancing the environment, placing a protective bubble on our locale, and defending us from evil influences. Carmen was trying to explain to me what he was saying each time he came to us and moved his hands around our forms, sort of like on the outer edge of our aura, wrapping an invisible ribbon around us. Always speaking to Sr. Padre (the Father), San Pedro (Saint Peter), and Madre Maria (Mother Mary), asking them to hold us and protect us from the evil power, and making an eternal bond for us.

My take on all of this was that we drank the cactus juice to open our minds, lending more susceptibility to the influences of spirituality and the universe, and it did. I could feel a sensation around my body which was neither physical nor carnal, more like a vibration.

Don Alejandro was circling the altar then facing the fire, looking up into the night sky. He seemed a bit agitated. He was calling out names and appeared to be challenging someone. He turned his back on the sky and circled the altar again, spreading his arms wide, with his head down, concentrating on the altar and the figures. Chanting the names again and praying to them.

## CHASING THE DREAM

At this point, Carmen and I noticed that the statues were moving, almost like dancing or swaying. Maria was rocking the baby, San Pedro was dancing, and everything was trembling. The Don grabbed the bottle of Florida water, drank, and sprayed it into the air.

Immediately, he grabbed the two swords which had been stuck in the ground, twirled around, and swung them up high above his head, ready for combat. It appeared that he was really fighting someone or something; the metal swords were sparking and flaming against the night sky. This slashing and clanging of swords continued for a few minutes. Carmen and I sat frozen in time. The statues were writhing around, the fire blazed higher, and the candle flames were gyrating wildly in the swirling wind.

Then, twirling around, face pointed toward the heavens, the Don stood silently with his mighty swords held high, but all other movement had ceased. He slowly lowered the swords to his sides. He turned, shuffled to the altar, inserted the swords into the ground, and bowed his head. Carmen and I were spellbound, and we just sat there, waiting for the next scene. This was quite the flick. We'd be remembering this one forever.

Remember, Carmen was not able to get any of that cactus juice down, but later, when she recalled her experience to me, it paralleled mine exactly.

I told Carmen that I felt different, lighter, happier, and she said that she felt the same, like a rejuvenation of our souls. Well, for my soul, I no longer had the parasitic demon sinking its teeth into my psyche. I already knew the Don had been true to his word and had driven the evil spirit into the night sky.

The sun was peeking over the mountains by the time we finished the ceremony. Carmen and I headed back to Chiclayo to meet her sister in our hotel room. She was watching Carmen's daughter, Naylita. We had vanilla crackers in the car for breakfast.

## NORMAN WALTERS

● ● ●

Just to let you know, the ceremony worked. Carmen and I began sharing a normal relationship. I would say a normal life also, but I won't. With my schedule of "to the lodge on Sunday, home on Friday," my life was anything but normal. You could almost say that I was living a double life. We married in June of 1996, a grand gala. Fun was had by all!

PART 4
# THE BAPTISM OF THE LODGE

*Rio Yarapa*
*1994*

# FIVE

**NORMAL LIFE FOR US WAS** kind of disjointed. We lived for the weekends, and other than my Saturdays in the office, the three of us were inseparable, with long rides on my motorcycle (the little one almost always fell asleep wedged between us), ice cream at Ari's, cold coconuts to drink, on the only *carretera* (highway), and eating together at all meals.

Building went on in the jungle, and the dream became more and more of a reality with every week that passed. We were getting closer to opening. Bungalows were built, main bathrooms were built with real septic tank dispersion underground. There was no waste going into the river...a whole new concept for the jungle. I just could not see discharging our waste into the river with the village of Puerto Miguel below us.

I had just come from living in Nevada near Virginia City (that old western town depicted in many a TV series), where all the gold mining had taken place in the mid-1800s. The last spec house we built had to have a $10,000 water purification system for the inhabitants to be able to use the water (not drink it, just *use* it). The well was drilled 2,500 feet deep through solid granite, and was so full of arsenic and other residual poisons that I thought we might lose the investment.

That was not the only problem. It had to have a septic tank for solid waste (no city sewage services in the mountains). I had to work with the engineers to create a septic system that would function with no percolation in solid granite. I did it, and we sold the house.

The jungle was sort of like the same problem, with all the flooding and the clay soil. Hundreds and hundreds of feet of underground, four-inch perforated drainage pipe from the concrete septic tanks deep into the jungle. I designed and built six systems, which worked even when the land was totally flooded (no clouded water either). All the toilets flushed, showers and sinks drained, and I was amazed.

• • •

That year, 1994, we had our first guests, a sixtyish couple booked by our agency, Eco Expeditions in Miami, as a test to see how we were stacking up. The water was still up, covering all of our earth. Our elevated walkways, which snaked around the grounds (the only path through the water to the main gathering building), were lit up with our flaming lamps. It was night, and it was dinnertime, so I blew the *churro* (a very large jungle snail) shell to alert the guests that it was time to eat.

Shortly after, we all heard a big splash and a loud yelp from the shadows. I ran out and saw the man standing in about eighteen inches of water off of the edge of the walkway. His wife was standing there with her hands over her mouth, laughing. He had not worn his glasses and did not jig when the walkway jogged. He walked right off the edge and into the water. No harm, no foul, thank God. We had not finished the railings on that part of the walkway yet. Murphy's Law to be certain.

## CHASING THE DREAM

All went well, though. They loved the canoe trips through the jungle, the early morning bird watching, after-dinner black caiman (crocodile) searches on the river by flashlight, the menu of local dishes, the guides—everything was good. We passed the litmus test with flying colors.

It was about this time that we decided to build a mode of transportation for getting groups to and from the lodge. We were still in our first stages of preparation for guests, so deciding what we wanted to build was maybe a bit of backward thinking. Throwing this back and forth for a while, Lawrence and I finally decided on a fifty-foot double-decked transport with a pilot's cabin, bar, bathroom, observation deck, and sitting lounge in the hold, all wood. We searched for a boat builder with a reputation and actual boats—in service—that we could check out.

We found a builder in a small area by Tamshiyacu, called Panguana. Walter lived with his mother and brother on the bank of the Rio Amazonas—easy boat launching. The day we went to visit him he had just finished a boat and launched it. Unfortunately, we weren't able to observe this, but it didn't really matter, for we had seen a few of his boats, and they were definitely river-worthy.

Here I would like to give homage to a woman who brought two boys into this world, lost her husband, and raised two daughters and two sons, boat builders, on the banks of the Amazon River.

*My drawing of Walter's mother, 1999*

I'd like to relate a poignant story that is sad but true: The mayor of Iquitos, thinking that it would be a great idea to bring a noteworthy celebration to his city on New Year's Eve, purchased the type of fireworks that we see in the U.S.—a shitload of them.

At midnight, he unleashed a spectacle no one had ever seen or even heard of in the history of Iquitos. Of course, all the villages surrounding Iquitos as far as forty to fifty miles away heard and saw the display. How beautiful it was for the people of Iquitos and the developed areas around.

The only problem was the surrounding undeveloped jungle villages. Walter's mother, who was old, thought it was the end of the world—Armageddon. She had a massive heart attack and died. I was told that many of the jungle people were scared and did not understand what was happening.

The evangelistic missionaries had preached that the end was near, and the booms and explosive light displays convinced the local jungle inhabitants that the end of days was upon them.

I had made a sketch of the boat we wanted him to build, kind of copying the profile of another boat he had built. That would be where the similarities would end. We had quite a few ideas of what we wanted. Juan translated for us, and after mucho negotiations he was able to understand what we were trying to accomplish. Our boat would not be for cargo, it would be for passengers. We agreed on a price and what materials we would be responsible for supplying.

I would work out the base of the hull, or the *plantilla*. I wanted to make it out of itauba wood, a very hard heartwood that we found in the jungle sometimes. Hundred-year wood at the least. We were lucky that someone had a plantilla of itauba that I could buy. It sped up the process not having to find it, drag it out of the jungle, carve it, and deliver it to Walter. We agreed to supply all the wood planks, tar, fiber chinking, galvanized steel sheets, nails, paint, and everything else that it takes to build a floating wooden boat.

It was a good day when I delivered the plantilla to Walter. He could actually start the construction. The wood was already sitting there. The fasteners were there, and all it would take was the master's touch to create our dream boat.

*Plantilla of itauba wood*

*First planks on the plantilla*

*The ribs of the hull*

*Walter, Norman, and Lawrence*

*Taking shape*

*The finished product, "Yacumama I"*

This was a truly magnificent boat. Perfect equilibrium, comfortable seats, booze, bathroom, and a twelve-hour voyage to the lodge. *WHAT?* A twelve-hour trip in and twelve back? That information is right. All of the first groups accepted it, but for me it was a little tedious, and everyone arrived drunk. I sold a lot of beer, but after a while we decided to make something else: a boat that cut the time down substantially. My plan was to build an aluminum boat, sleek and fast, and sell the "Big Baby." It would hold twenty-four guests, though not quite as comfortable, and arrive in three and a half hours. Now that's what I was talkin' about!

*24 passengers, comfortably*

I sold the wooden ship, *Yacumama I*, to a new acquaintance of mine, Gerald (my friend to this day, owner of the Yellow Rose of Texas, an exceptional restaurant and sports bar in the Plaza de Armas, Iquitos, Peru), who had a fishing lodge at that time for the hearty ones: peacock bass fishing in the lakes.

• • •

Federico, our mastermind at Eco Expeditions (the Miami booking agency), had wrangled four pro photographers, friends of his from *National Geographic* magazine, to photograph at the lodge for our new travel brochure.

They came for two weeks and photographed everything: flora, fauna, insects, reptiles, and the lodge itself. It was really cool how they set up for shoots.

## CHASING THE DREAM

*The photographic group*

We all learned a lot and had the greatest times together. We even used some of their shots for our new brochure.

I kept a guest book from the beginning, which turned out to be a very self-appreciating synopsis of what we had done: creating one of the very first true ecotourism lodges, complete with solar-powered lights, recycling, and eco-sewage disposal. Federico, in our Miami office, organized familiarization tours for all the Peruvian and Miami travel agents. These "fam" tours spanned months in 1994, during which we sharpened our guest skills and I honed my dissertation (for the Doctorate of Tourism, LOL), which I gave to every new group arriving.

Lawrence was invited to the first touristic eco-lodge symposium in Lima, Peru, and gave an "on target" talk of what it all really meant (the golden tongue again). We were inundated with questions of how, where, when, and who. I also kept a file on articles written about us in all the major travel mags, which actually included newspapers and magazine articles from Lima, Peru. Surprising!

*Federico and me in the hotel*

Enough of this blowing-our-horn bullshit. Let's get down to some real nitty-gritty. How about *POACHERS?*

**PART 5**

# POACHERS

*Rio Yarapa*
*1995*

# SIX

**WE HAD A BIT OF DOWNTIME** between the early groups, and sometimes (just *sometimes*) I stayed in Iquitos with my newly formed family for a few days. We had dinners, and I became acquainted with all the extended family extracts.

We were at one of those dinners when one of my assistants barged into the Chifa Wai Ming, our favorite Chinese restaurant, calling me aside.

"*Señor, una persona de tu lodge dijo que hay hombres cortando árboles en tu terreno.*"

Wow, men cutting trees on our land. I couldn't believe it, but I guessed I had to. I had been looking forward to this day with dread, and it had arrived. When I struck the deal with the Ag office for the land purchase, I had pleaded with them to help me try to control the poaching. After much ado, Sr. Padilla and the *jefe* of the department created a new department for me: *Guarda Bosque*, or "Forest Guard." I was given the power to protect the forest and animals, paralyze the actions of the poachers, confiscate their illegally obtained products, and turn the offenders over to the authorities.

*Forest Guard document*

Needless to say, the next morning I was on my way to the lodge. It was a big thing to cut down a 200-year-old tree, let alone 400- to 500-year-old ones. On my trip out I thought about the villager who had cut down one of our trees to extract a couple of liters of medicinal resin to sell for S/.100.00 (*soles*), or about $30 U.S. This was right after we started construction, and the 150-foot tree was close to the river—easy access.

I was returning from Iquitos after an extended weekend and saw the top branches and leaves obscuring the riverbank, extending twenty feet into the river. I knew who did it, and what he did was a normal

## CHASING THE DREAM

action of the jungle civilization that he lived in. Yes, it was illegal, but it was done, and it would have just made the villagers hate me if I were to ask for action against him. The kicker is: I had to send my guys to clean it up. He had chopped the three-and-a-half-foot-diameter tree down with an axe—gotta hand it to the guy. Got brass ones.

Thinking of that occurrence brought on another travesty that had made me cry:

I first discovered the *guacamayos*, or macaws, on a trip upriver with tourists. We'd always seen flocks of red and blue macaws flying around the lodge, but I had never seen them nesting. This time it was different. We had just started out from the lodge when our guide, Octavio, pointed out two red guacamayos flying overhead.

We always saw them in pairs; later, when the ornithologists started visiting the lodge, I learned that they are "till death do us part" birds. They mate for life and live thirty to fifty years in the wild. They reach sexual maturity at around three to four years old. When they nest the mother lays two to four eggs, then stays with the nest while the father protects her and brings her food. They will not mate again until the chicks have fledged and are on their own.

They were circling a very tall tree which appeared to have a large hole in its side approximately seventy-five feet up the trunk, probably occurring from a rotted branch. Octavio signaled to our motorist (boat driver) to slow down and cut the motor. We all watched while the birds circled a few times, and then one of them lit on the edge of the hole and disappeared inside. In a few seconds its head appeared out of the hole. The other bird lit on a branch above the hole. Octavio told us that we were experiencing the beginning of a new household in our neighborhood. He was always very good with tourists, lovable and funny.

In the next month (they incubate their eggs for about twenty-eight days), the mom's head never left the hole. We'd see the dad flying around, never with a flock, and sometimes sitting on the above branch. One time we actually saw him perched on the edge of the hole, feeding the mother, and another time preening her feathers. They became one of our many attractions, but for me, and for most of our guests, they were our very special neighbors.

One day, with a boat full of tourists, Octavio stopped the boat in front of the tree and pointed out that there were two little downy heads sticking out of the nest. Since most of the guests had binoculars around their necks, the conversations at lunch were all about the babies. A couple of the guests had cameras with telephoto lenses (no digital cameras or iPhones yet) so they would have a lasting memory of the event. Close up and personal.

As the weeks and months passed the babies grew and began getting color in their feathers, and mom was able to leave the nest a bit (a two-income family). We felt like they were part of our family; we were always keeping tabs on them and watching them grow.

Then the fledglings began standing on the edge of the nest, sort of trying their wings out, and mom and dad would be sitting on the above branch, watching them. I believe that the parents actually kept them from trying to fly until they knew that they could. A seventy-five-foot drop to the riverbank or into the water probably would not have been a good experience for them. They might not have even survived.

Octavio returned to the lodge from an excursion with our guests one afternoon and advised me that the babies were flying around the nest with the parents. I guessed that they were growing up and would all disappear soon. We were able to watch them for another few weeks. On one rainy day Octavio told me that they had left to be with the flock.

Wow, what a wonderful chapter in my life. By that time, I knew that they mated about once a year, so I was dreaming about them returning to take up residence in our tree again.

## CHASING THE DREAM

They did come back for two more years, and they were the tourists' delight both times. The third year Octavio told me that they were flying around the tree again, and I alerted the guests to what they would see for the next few days of their visit. The birds were still flying in and out of the flock, obviously getting ready to mate and take up the household again.

We were eating lunch after the guests' excursion upriver, conversing about the birds.

One guest said, "We saw the macaws today. They were perched on the branch above the hole in the tree. I believe she will enter the nest soon."

Everyone was smiling and imagining the details, I'm sure, of the birds' rare actions, when there was a very loud explosion upriver. I knew immediately what it was. I got up and met Octavio running to the dock. He looked at me with shock in his eyes. I called for our motorist, Eleodoro at that time, and the three of us jumped in my speedboat, *Yacuruna*. We sped off upriver, and as we rounded the bend, there on the bank stood a man with a red mass in his hands.

He was a disabled man who had come to live in Puerto Miguel with his wife and four children about six months earlier. I asked him what the hell he was thinking, and he replied that he could feed his family and sell the feathers (totally illegal) to buy clothes for his kids.

Well…I took him to the police depot in Puerto Miguel and made a complaint against him, but I never followed it up and pursued it no more. WTF does a person do in a situation like that? I could have just killed him and dropped him in the river, or beat him to a pulp to teach him a lesson, but in reality, what is the most important thing to a man? His family? Yes, I believe so, and he was just thinking of a way to help his family survive.

I returned to the lodge with a heavy heart, gave the heart-wrenching news to the guests and the staff, then retired to my house to grieve.

The hardest part for me was seeing the male flying around the tree for the next couple of weeks, alone. Then he was gone. *Om Mani Padme Hum.*

• • •

Here we go, back to reality. We were pulling up to the poachers' floating dock—I was forming a plan of how to confront the poachers. This was my first date with them, and I wanted to make a good impression. I rounded up four of my biggest men (a real chore, seeing that Peruvians are not known to be big), four loaded shotguns, my pump riot gun, and my .38 Special strapped to my side. Hopefully that would do it.

I did not want to threaten them at first, so the guns went down. I knew there would be a confrontation, though; how not? They were blatantly stealing our trees.

As we motored up I saw the surprise on their faces, and I noticed the raft they were making of the felled trees to float downriver to Iquitos (and sell). I noticed that a few of them had old shotguns in their hands, pointed at the ground. This was not what I needed.

I asked, "*¿Donde esta tu jefe?*" (Where is your boss?)

Carlos stepped forward, a man I knew from another pueblo on the Ucayali River close to us.

"*¿Por qué estas cortando árboles de Yacumama?*" I queried. (Why are you cutting Yacumama trees?)

He sneered at me and said, "*Estos árboles son nuestros tambien!*" (These trees are ours too.)

"*No, Carlos, esto es propiedad privada. Hemos hablado sobre esto, y los pueblos acordaron no cortar árboles de Yacumama.*" (This is private property. We have talked about this, and the villages agreed not to cut Yacumama trees).

## CHASING THE DREAM

He looked at me and sneered, shaking his head side to side, uttering one word: "NO."

His men seemed to catch the vibe and started looking very nervous, fiddling with their guns. I gave the order to hold still and told Eleodoro to back up quickly and take off. He did! No one on either side discharged their firearm; thank the Great Spirit for that one. I looked at my guys, and they had that deer in the headlights look. Scared shitless but energized. I didn't notice any wet pants, so they made the grade.

When we got back to the lodge I invited them all to share a big *cerveza* with me. I told them that they did well, no one discharged their weapons, and we all came away alive and well. I had to ask them, though, "Would you pull the trigger if you had to?"

They all looked at each other, got shit-eating grins on their faces, sort of puffed up a bit, and nodded their heads up and down. I didn't really believe them, but maybe they believed themselves.

I radioed Iquitos and told my office to contact INRENA, the department for protecting the flora and fauna. They would come out if I gave them gas, which I always did. They arrived the next day at lunchtime. How apropos—I guess I was right to make extra food. Two forest police were with them, dressed in their SWAT-type uniforms with automatic rifles, radios and helmets—the whole nine yards.

Over lunch, I showed them my authorization to halt illegal activity and confiscate the illegally obtained products. I explained the situation to them, omitting the gun play, because only my guns were registered and licensed. They had paperwork to confiscate the trees, which belonged to us, and they asked what I wanted to do with them. I said I would think about it.

After lunch, they piled into their boat and we piled into ours, and off we went. The only things missing were our guns. Probably better that way.

We arrived at the tree raft, and the men were still there. I could hear chainsaws in the forest, and they only came alive when the forest police presented themselves and the INRENA representative called a stop to all activity. Carlos told them that he was commissioned to cut here by the concession he applied and paid for in the Department of Agriculture and INRENA in Iquitos. My office had given INRENA copies of the land titles that proved Carlos was on our land and his documents were fake, and it was time for me to leave the scene. The police were taking them into custody.

I was contacted later and asked if I wanted to press charges, and what did I want to do with the wood? This was a terrible situation to be in. No, I was not going to press charges. Carlos had to deliver the trees downriver to Puerto Miguel; they had to promise not to trespass and cut logs again (remember what Jesus Christ was supposed to have said, "Go and sin no more"); it would go on record with the police; and if they did try again, I would consider putting them in jail. SO THERE!

(Guess what? They did the same thing two more times, and their sons continued into the twenty-first century with the same activities. I busted them in 2014 over a huge operation eight hours up the river, at the top of our property, with the same ultimatum: Next time you go to jail. In 2017 the sons did it again, and no one alerted me in the U.S. until it was too late. I ordered the police out, and the boys escaped with the wood in the night.

I gave the wood, like always, to Puerto Miguel—they could cut it into usable dimensions with chainsaws and benefit—they'd probably sell it to a mill, though. Still, the pueblo would benefit, maybe?

The reason I say that is experience in the field or once bitten, twice shy. I'll tell you all about it:

When we were still young and full of philanthropic dreams, my partner, in one of his speeches to the pueblo, had promised a chicken

## CHASING THE DREAM

and a dozen eggs every month to every family in Puerto Miguel (Hoover won his presidency with words close to that). How would we achieve it? Well, I am the one who had to figger it out. You know, "rubber meeting the road."

After way too much time had passed and everyone was on my ass for the chickens and eggs, I had a town meeting with the villagers.

I will do this in English:

I started out, "Does anyone remember Lawrence's words about the chickens and eggs?" (I wasn't telling a joke, and please do not get confused.)

About a hundred hands went up, most of the adults in the village, and there was a roar of everyone trying to talk at once. I told Esteban to settle them down, and I would call on hands. Okay. I called on ten different people and received ten different stories, but they all ended the same: a chicken and a dozen eggs every month for every family.

Well, I couldn't change it, so I asked, "Where can I build a chicken farm close to your village, and who will live there to take care of it?" (For it was a very large responsibility).

Murmur, murmur, murmur. More murmuring. Finally the *teniente gobenador*, like a mayor, stood up and spoke.

"There is a man who has a *chacra*, farm, that he is not using, and it is big. He is a widowed man, and his name is Filemon. He will help you build it and live there to protect it."

At that time I still remembered Filemon as the man in the Speedo, guzzling *aguardiente* and pulling our lumber out of the sunken cargo boat. What a guy! Okay, that sounded good to me. Anything to get things rolling, because I was signing months of my life away.

I grew up in the Midwestern part of the country. When my father made a deal and shook hands, it was a binding contract. He completed the work, was paid, and life went on. A man's word was what he was made of, and unfortunately, here in the jungles of Peru, there were a few times when I had to fulfill promises that I never would have made. This was one of them. I lived here and had to keep the word that wasn't really mine.

Forty-five days later, with a crew of ten men, I had the land cleared, the henhouse built, the run fenced in, roosts and laying stations ready, Filemon's shack finished, 200 hens ready to grow into layers, another 150 for meat, ten roosters to make new chickens (for the meat), and a balanced feed that I picked up each week in Iquitos, for them all to eat. Done!

Well, not quite. I decided to plant papayas, bananas, cocona, and yuca to help augment the villagers' diets. Everything was going well, the chicks grew into hens, the roosters had their way with them, eggs appeared, and I was on my way to fulfilling the vow.

Filemon was doing a stellar job; we were getting fruit and eggs from the chacra. There were 350 hens, and I made the decision that the time was right to make the donation to the village elders. A town meeting was called—I had the papers drawn up in Iquitos—and you can believe me now, everyone was there. They arrived walking, stumbling, limping, even crawling, but they arrived to hear the news.

There were approximately a hundred-plus families living in Puerto Miguel. One family, the powerful branch of the tree, ran everything: government, bar, and *bodega* (food store). The three essentials.

It was a great celebration, with the mayor and other officials signing the agreement that the farm was to be for the betterment of the people in the pueblo of Puerto Miguel, and it was not to be used for self-gain, commercialism, or power struggles. It was written into the registry book, typed (with carbon paper) into a document. I signed, the mayor signed, the registrar signed, the assessor signed, I even had a few stray dogs sign (sorry). It was rubber-stamped ten times, held,

## CHASING THE DREAM

kissed, spit at (yes, there were a few non-believers), and retired to the pueblo's labyrinthine records.

I was relieved of duty, mustered out, hugged everyone, smiled (showing my teeth), jumped in the *Yacuruna*, waved, and I was geography. Just a touristic jungle lodge owner/manager again. I felt a huge weight lifted from my shoulders. When I arrived in Iquitos on Friday, I immediately called to give Lawrence the good news. The chicken and egg fiasco was over for us. You are welcome, thank you very much!

***Just to tidy up, I feel that I should let you know...***

About a month and a half later, I was in my usual station looking out on the river, drinking a beer, thinking about how we were advancing and the mountains that I must climb, when my guard came to me to proclaim, "You have visitors."

Three of the women from the village entered the building, and I offered them seats. I called to my waiter to bring *refresco*, and asked, "What's up?" I was surprised because I didn't have many visitors from the village; when I did it was trouble.

After all the greetings and cordialities the spokesperson, a lady I'd known since the beginning, began the conversation, "We have discovered that the chicken farm is gone. The powerful families of the pueblo took all the chickens, dismantled the buildings, and it is gone."

That was a real waker-upper!

I was at attention, asking, "How did this happen?"

It appears that everything just started disappearing until there was nothing, and because the chacra was deeper in the jungle nothing was noticed. Sort of like a magic trick. Oh, I'd bet it was a trick, all right. I was afraid of this, and I had voiced my opinions very strongly from the beginning. Now it was a reality, and I could do nothing about it.

I walked to the farm and took in the spectacle in front of me. Splintered boards, pieces of chicken wire, broken feed buckets—that was all there was. I talked with the authorities who had signed the document, and nobody knew anything. Filemon said things just started disappearing at night. Uh-huh! A great big dead end. I did hear of a new stall opening in the *Nauta Mercado*, about two hours away by boat, to buy chickens and eggs, but try to prove that!

I only had to think, *What goes around, comes around.* I am sure that it does. It is just hard to see sometimes.

**PART 6**
# CALIFORNIA DREAMIN'
*Petaluma*
*1970*

# SEVEN

**I KNOW IT HAS BEEN A LONG WHILE** since I've talked about my bubba and me (in the early days), but I figured that this was a good break from all the joys and woes experienced in the preceding chapters.

We had been a little too long in Indiana—lichen growing on my brain cells. I needed to get some stimulus from the outside world. Larry and I picked a beautiful day to start hitching. We were finally going to California to hook up with our New York friend, Thayer, the beauty in the fringed white buckskin pants whom we met in Central Park in 1969.

Larry and I took a very enlightening trip to NYC in 1969, opening our eyes to a brand new "Brave World," which we knew existed, just not where we lived. We had a watered-down version in Goshen, Indiana—not quite reaching the edge of the cliff where we were known to hang out.

When we parted from her she was on her way to California with her then-boyfriend, Cosmo, a great guy, and we were on our way, hitchhiking back to Indiana with our tails between our legs. Sort of embarrassing to admit, but it was what it was, and it is what it is. We finally found our mojo again, and one day Larry exclaimed, "Let's go to California!"

I'd been spinning my wheels, making etchings at Notre Dame University, playing my songs at a small venue, and writing a bad, bad book, while Larry was silk-screening and selling T-shirts with images of Jesus Christ on them. This existence was easy enough to leave, believe me. The sun was out, blue skies surrounded us, and we had not a care in the world.

It was only a 2,500-mile hitch, and we decided to take the north route, I-80, because it was still early and the snow should not have been falling yet. It was the fastest route to California. Everything was good, nice people picking us up (except the guy with all the white powder on his lap).

Thayer was living in Santa Cruz, and our last ride took us to her doorstep—talk about luck. I always carried the map, marking our path through the highway labyrinth we encountered. No Google Maps.

She lived in a cute little cottage on a hill overlooking Santa Cruz. Quite nice. She had just purchased a ten-acre spread in the middle of millions of acres of dairy farmland. I guess it was a caretaker's property in the day.

She showed us pictures and told us stories of her life. She was doing well, had her son, a new boyfriend, a new life, and us, LOL. Actually, having us wasn't a bad thing for her. She couldn't spend all of her time there; it was very remote, and she was part of the "Dead family," traveling a lot. Get the picture?

We had been on a visiting trip, planning to end up in Seattle. We'd heard that Jay, the lead guitarist we had in NYC, was living there, and I really wanted to talk to him.

Thayer asked us if we would like to stay at the ranch (which she had named Frog Holler) to help her keep the workers in line. They

## CHASING THE DREAM

were clearing the grounds, ripping out hundreds of rabbit hutches, inner fences, and wild bushes that had been taking over the property. We did have to go to Seattle first, and promised her that we would be back in two weeks.

We all went to Frog Holler the next day, and it was really beautiful, nestled in the middle of a lush valley with rolling hills on all sides. There was a half-mile driveway, a gate, a bubbling creek that ran down the back hill with long grass blowing in the wind, and dogs. Big dogs. Great Dane big.

There was a lot of activity at the ranch, guys tearing things down, ripping blackberry bushes out, working and repairing an early twentieth century Victorian gabled three-story house (gingerbread and bric-a-brac intact). It was quite a spectacle. She told us that we could live in the house, help out a bit, and help watch her son while she was on trips. Sure, we were fancy-free and had no obligations, responsibilities, or needs. The brother of her boyfriend was doing the repair work on the house, and we could help if we wanted. I was still writing songs, playing guitar, and performing once in a while, so it seemed like a great deal—chill for a while. Her son was totally cool; we had met and watched him when he was younger in NYC; no problem there.

We entered the house, and it smelled old and closed up, but Thayer had furnished it with some of her Oriental rugs, antique furniture, Tiffany lamps, and of course incense burning all around, so it wasn't hard on the eyes or nose. I looked at Larry; Larry looked at me. We nodded, and he said, "Sure, Thayer, we'd love to. Thanks."

We would hitch right back here in two weeks, call her when we arrived, and she would come up to arrange all the particulars. We hugged, shook hands with all the workers; she explained our situation and then dropped us off on Highway 101 going north. This would be a cinch, only 800 miles.

We did want to visit a bunch of Goshen girls that had moved up to Washougal, Washington. They had a nice secluded farmhouse that was close to a creek with a beautiful waterfall, and it was just a few miles off of our route. They were very good friends, and we hadn't seen them for quite a while. Some of our buds had stopped by earlier in the year and said it was a great pit stop between San Francisco and Seattle. Great for skinny-dipping.

It was; we relaxed, swam, laughed, talked old times, ate some good grub, smoked, drank some Liebfraumilch wine (no Boones Farm or Strawberry Hill for me anymore), and were on our way again.

We pulled into Seattle in the early afternoon, located Jay's street, and went the wrong way on it (east). We had to turn around after knocking on a door and no one had ever heard of him. Hmmm, wrong end of the street. We walked the twenty blocks back to the same address but west, and he answered the door. He looked good and was still playing his Gibson Hummingbird guitar.

We rapped for a while, went out to get a bite to eat, came back, talked 'til the early hours and crashed. The morning was kind of overcast and felt like Northeastern weather. It had been five days since we left California, and Larry decided to call Thayer to let her know that we were with Jay and all was fine. Everyone still had telephones in their houses back then, but not Jay; Larry had to go to the corner to call on a payphone. He came back too quickly, and I figured that she had not answered the phone until I saw his face.

"The old house burnt to the ground two nights ago. Thayer didn't have a number to reach us, and she was frantic. Her boyfriend is on a trip, his brother Patrick was working on the electrical and might have caused a short circuit," he said. Then his eyes started watering up and I feared for the worst, but he continued, "Nicky (her son) was on the third floor asleep (my heart sank), and Patrick ran through the fire,

# CHASING THE DREAM

grabbed him and jumped out the window to the second floor roof, then to the first floor roof, and then to the ground. Everyone is safe, but the house is completely gone. Everything is gone, including all the stuff we left there…your guitar!"

Wow, I had only had that guitar for a few months. I had bought it at Rex's Record Rack in Goshen, on layaway, paying weekly, anxiously awaiting the day that I would have my brand-spanking-new Martin D-28. What a beauty, and what a sound. It was gone. I'd get another guitar.

Nicky was safe, and Patrick was a hero. Yay, he saved our boy (whom we would be caring for over the next two years).

We cut our trip short and got on the road by noon. Luckily the Great Spirit was with us, and we arrived at Frog Holler twenty hours later. Larry called Thayer, alerting her to the fact that we were at the ranch and that we were figuring out where we were going to sleep. She told us not to worry; they were going to buy tents and renovate the sheep shed into a house. Boy, that was going to be a job.

Larry and I had a big tent, probably a ten-foot-by-twelve-foot, and we had a heater for when it started getting cold (which would be soon). There was a command tent for the workers, and I had to dig a latrine in the side of the hill, build an enclosure, and maintain it. This was a lot different than living in a beautiful Victorian house with all the necessary means to be normal. It was a while before we got electric lights, a kitchen stove, and refrigerator installed in the sheep shed. The inside floor was lower than the ground level, so it flooded every time it rained. We had to dig a trench all the way around the building and form up for a concrete wall to keep the water out. It was a bitch, and it took a while. Larry and I ended up in the tent for the first part of the winter. Northern California winters get pretty cold; it even snowed. When we finally moved into the shed it was pretty cramped with Larry, me, Nicky some of the time, and her Harlequin Great Dane, but it was better than a poke in the eye!

There were lonely times, you know, when work was hard, not much enjoyment was to be had. I daydreamed (wrapped up in a down mummy bag in the tent, thirty-five-degree weather with slushy rain falling outside) about other times when things were not the best but way better than this.

I recalled the times in Goshen with my "brutha from anutha mutha" Jim: We lived together, worked, and hung like two guys on the edge. It would have been a pretty shitty existence if it had not been for our friends. We were the rebels, and we were the guys that the muthas did not want their daughters to be made muthas with.

I remember one night when we were all having a good time in our little house by the tracks (or whatever that division was in the street), smokin' a bit, drinkin' a bit, and having a hilarious time, someone (I always thought it was Jim) set up a camera and snapped a picture. It always was one of my very faves.

"Those were the days, my friend. We thought they'd never end." A person never thinks of the future when they are living the life, but that has its drawback also. As I've said before: My sister always said that if I fell in the shit I would come out smelling like a rose. Well, that was true, but only because of my surfing ability, and after a bunch

*Self Portrait, Janet, me, Kathy, Lucia, and Jim (up)*

## CHASING THE DREAM

of years and shit stains those roses may actually be turning into potpourri. What lovely memories. All of the shit times turn into memories eventually, so why dwell on them and worry?

• • •

We made a shower out of old clear glass sliding balcony doors. It wasn't a bad life; we had all the money we needed to buy everything organic and natural. That was the main "good deal" for me. We just lived and built and took care of Nicky.

He had to be seven years old by then, and he attended the valley's one-room school. Christmas time came along, and I guess he mentioned to the teacher that he lived with musicians, so she told him she wanted to talk to us. Well, "us" was me, so I went to see what was on her mind. I had met her and seen her many times from driving the boy to school in the morning and picking him up in the afternoon. She was a settled, older lady, pleasant-looking, a pleasant person, and good with the kids (Nicky didn't hate her). When I picked him up, I went in. She immediately smiled at me and shook my hand.

"Would you play the music for our Christmas program?" she asked.

That caught me off guard. Hair to my shoulders, a beard, and a mind that ticked at a much different rate than the Chilean dairy farmers in our "Chileno Valley" (Northern California), I responded, "Are you sure?"

"Oh yes, it would be wonderful. I usually play the piano, but it is so old, and now it's out of tune."

"Oh. When would we practice?" I asked. "I can come pretty much any time, any day."

"We only have three weeks, so why not tomorrow after lunch? That would be around 1:00 in the afternoon."

"Okay, you got it!" I said, smiling.

I knew Christmas songs from playing them with my mother, but I never imagined that I would be doing this. The next day I showed up on time, and we began.

I played while the children (ages five to twelve) sang all the old standbys for Christmas. They got better and better, and by the time the program came around—stellar! I showed up, dragging Nicky along (it was the first time he had ever done anything like that), met all the parents. They were Chilean men and women mostly, with a few whiteys sprinkled in.

We were already set up, so the kids took their places, pushing and shoving, and we began, "Silent night. Holy night. All is calm, all is bright…"

The parents clapped, laughed, and a good time was had by all. The parents appeared to love it, and afterward they thanked me for participating in the program. I was kind of blown away, you might say, but a bit proud too, that I could pull off such a feat and that no one threw tomatoes at me. I knew they were "packing," though—in their wives' purses. The teacher, Mrs. Crawford, made me promise to play the next year. I participated two years, and then I left the area, and so did Nicky.

The best thing about Christmas that year was that it almost felt like family. I was thinking, "I'm dreaming of a white Christmas…" but it didn't snow. Thayer commissioned me to make her man, whom we had gotten to know quite well, an incredible belt buckle. It was the head of a ram (he was an Aries), twenty-eight ounces of silver, with an opal for the seventh chakra.

*Belt buckle concept*

## CHASING THE DREAM

He gave Larry and me Martin guitars for Christmas, Larry a D-18 and me a D-35 with an S neck.

Christmas couldn't get much better than that! Could it?

## PART 7
# HERE COME DA GROUPS (AND SURPRISES)

*Yacumama Lodge*
*1995*

# EIGHT

**WE WERE IN THE INCREDIBLE YEAR** of 1995, the inception of everything we had been working for. This year would produce the fruits of our labor. We already had tentative bookings from Rainforest Health Project, the Children's Environmental Trust, Smithsonian, GreenTracks, as well as FITs (free independent travelers), families, and couples. It was looking to be a good year.

With 1995 being the "birth year" of RHP and CET, the groups were small, and our seven-bungalow accommodations worked out just fine. Each year after that we had to grow, grow, and grow more, until in 1999 I had built another nineteen bungalows and another separate bathroom with toilets and urinals (for women and men, just used differently), showers and lavatories.

We stretched into the jungle on elevated walkways. Because the main lodge and the main pasadiso were on a ridge and retreated into the swamp, the walkway started about eighteen inches above the ground and grew to five feet by the back bungalows. And believe me when I say, all walkways had railings!

We could sleep and feed seventy-two people (that was the largest group we ever had). It was a little tight; I decided that we never wanted a group that large again, and we didn't have one. It was really cool how everything fit together, though, like pieces of a puzzle.

*Yacumama's seating for 72 guests*

Carmen, Nayla, and I were living together at this time, and I leased the complete third floor of a building close to the city center. Pablo, my house guy, moved with us to be security when I wasn't there, which started being every week. I moved the office into the entry room at the end of the three flights of stairs to accommodate my desk, filing cabinets, and a waiting area for visiting employees. Many of the wives received their husbands' wages in the office.

Federico sent a close friend's son to help me out in the lodge. Colin was a good-looking blond German-Peruvian boy in his late twenties (he lived with us too…not good). I liked him, but what I really needed was help. Calls from the airport saying that there was no one to meet the guests, or the baggage wasn't on the cargo boat so it couldn't leave, were not what I needed to hear.

Before Colin arrived I was a one-man show. I picked guests up at the airport, accompanied them to the hotel, making sure every room

## CHASING THE DREAM

was okay. I gave a welcome talk, introduced them to the guides, laid out the activities for the day (city tour, lunch on them, check out the town, change money, and meet for dinner on me). I told them the time for breakfast at the hotel and the time for luggage in the lobby, and when pick-up was to go to our boats. It was a routine, which reversed when we returned six days later. After spending the week with them, orchestrating every meal, excursion, and minor problem, the last I saw of them was the butt swaying up the ramp stairs to the plane.

Now you see, help would have been welcomed.

I had four different assistants in a couple of years. None worked out. We even brought my nephew Bill, son Luke, and Lawrence's son Aaron at different times; one or two of them came every summer to help with the CET kid's groups. They were better than the adult helpers…they really liked to talk to the pretty girls though, LOL.

I pray this is not getting too tedious for you all. I hate it when an author tries to fill up pages by repeating things or saying the same things in a different way…just eating up pages and my time. I am reading a book now by a very famous writer—but wait, there is another person's name in much smaller print below his. Does that mean the famous man did not write the book? It certainly isn't the style of writing I am accustomed to with the "big guy," and I usually get kissed before I get…you-know-what!

I guess it is all about money now. What do you think? I've already lost interest in his book. I am just worried that I will not be able to stuff all the rest of what happened to me (and us) in the next eight years, and then the other sixteen on top of it, in *THIS* book.

I believe this is the best time to explain what these two major groups, CET and RHP, were trying to achieve with their trips to the Amazon. As I've said, there is a great need for young people to understand the importance that a rainforest has in the scheme of things, like life. The Children's Environmental Trust was started by two men with a vision, Jim Cronk and Doug Larkin, but they had a slew of people to thank. The focus was on kids eleven to fourteen, middle school, old enough to know a few things but not set in their ways yet. They could still learn and act, which many of them did. We probably hosted 600—700 kids, more or less, in the years we were open.

Those two men put an exceptional amount of their time and money into starting this program. They came to talk to us at the construction site in late summer of 1993, I believe, or maybe 1994. We made a deal, and we took it as far as we could.

Professors from major universities came with the groups to demonstrate the symbiotic nature of the rainforest. They all came—bird, fish, reptile, insect, native plant—you name the "-ologist" and we had them. I learned a lot just listening to the classes. We also offered classes called "Arts and Crafts of the Amazon" as well as "A Shaman's Herbal Handbag."

*Arts and crafts with women from Puerto Miguel*

For the crafts, we brought in and paid women from the village (not always the very best, because I believed that anyone who was trying to make a living for their family deserved a shot at it) to come to the lodge and teach the kids and instructors the art of weaving and bracelet making.

*Jan Probst with Beltran Pacaya, Artist*

This is where Jan Probst from CET really shined. She was so attuned to the arts and the promotion of the crafts.

After I created the Artisan's Guild, I tried to get a pottery branch started for national and international distribution and sales. I wanted to help these people, with their genuine talents, rise above the stigmas and poverty that they existed in. I asked my potter friend, Dan Baer, to design me a kiln to fire their pottery (he fires his pottery with hardwood) because they fired their pots *in* the actual fire. It does okay, but they do crack and break easier.

I did learn that the grey clay from our area in the Amazon River Basin has been used for the space shuttle tile skin (to combat the heat from reentry to our atmosphere), so their materials were excellent.

Unfortunately, when Dan hipped me to the quantity of wood it takes to actually fire good pottery in a kiln, we bombed out. They would be deforesting, and the logistics would be insurmountable. Another one bites the dust! Good thing I hadn't changed anything in their culture.

## NORMAN WALTERS

*Sarita making a clay pot*

At least the weaving and carving aspects of the guild were great successes. The CET groups of youngsters helped the village tremendously. The village even built a building for the weekly craft fairs I created, with a big help from the women of the village of Puerto Miguel.

The children of the village had clothing and food. The mothers had food to eat to produce milk for their babies, because the women received the money directly. This was different than their men working because the money that I paid the men was spent on alcohol. The women got nothing to take care of the family. That is why I worked to empower the women and created the Artist's Guild, liberating and raising their self-esteem, and it worked!

This was an ongoing moneymaker for them. The groups spent on an average $300 to $1,000, depending on the size and zeal of the group, at weekly craft fairs lasting until our final group of CET in the early summer of 2001, with Jim introducing us to a new group from Castine, Maine.

## CHASING THE DREAM

*Weekly craft fair in Puerto Miguel*

*The best basket weaver*

*Beltran's carvings*

# NORMAN WALTERS

*Castine, Maine, group fishing with Octavio in Huvos Lake*

*Carmen helping with "Pen Pal Letters"*

Little did we know in those glorious days what was lurking around the corner. There is no preparation for the unknown, so we merrily rolled along.

• • •

The Yarapa River people in 1992 were a governmentally forgotten people. The new president, Alberto Fujimori, was slowly trying to incorporate and merge the jungle people into the society. I remember seeing a poster in the Iquitos Airport: a photograph of a tribally dressed man with others behind him, and the message was, *"Somos Peruanos tambien"* (We're Peruvians too).

When we started helping the villages by building schools, giving medical assistance, employment, benefits, and helping with their personal problems, they viewed us as a lifesaver. One of our "fam" tour groups were journalists and TV reporters from Lima. They interviewed the people of Puerto Miguel and were surprised when a spokesperson replied that Yacumama had given them more support than the government.

## CHASING THE DREAM

*Norman, Ramon (our local Shaman, now departed), and Patty*

Never did we want to dis the Peruvian government, but it was true; we did sink some serious dough into the area.

So when Patty Webster and Sadie Bronson came by our riverfront lodge in 1993 or '94, when we under construction, and laid out their ideas for a medical group that would help the people of many villages, coming back a few times a year, keeping records, and trying to raise the standard of health, we fell right in. We worked out a deal, and they had their first group in 1995, or maybe the end of '94. Like with all groups, there were great times, good times, and questionable times.

Rainforest Health Project was the hope and salvation for the villages. They were a no-BS organization; the rubber met the road with them. The lodge was used as a transient hospital. People were lying around with IV tubes in their arms, looking like death warmed over. It was a time in our lives that could not be compared to anything today.

Rainforest Health Project did eventually go down, and there was a vacant space while Patty tried to pick up the pieces. She did with the help of some of her old colleagues. Then there was Amazon Promise, and everything was back on track. She picked it up with all the records, and it was pretty seamless. I have nothing but admiration for the guts and gristle it took to do it all over again. I've walked that highway a few times.

• • •

*Shaman Humberto with a group*

As I mentioned earlier, we offered native medicinal plant classes to the groups also. This class consisted of walks through the jungle (close to the lodge), a bit of collection, and explanations as to what was found and what the plants were good for. Our shaman also brought special plants to display and identify. The medical group, RHP, picked up on this and began offering the classes to their volunteers at the lodge.

For the herbal bag I brought out my favorite Iquitos shaman, Humberto Huinapi (the Great Spirit rest his soul), who helped and made life easier for me with flower baths and herbal chants. He brought some semblance of peace and serenity to my life. I wish I had a recording of his chants. He made herbal whisk brooms, which he shook and lightly touched the body with while whistling the most simple and beautiful tunes—captivating!

*Humberto Huinapi and Norman in "the day"*

# NINE

**IN THIS MAGICAL YEAR** of new beginnings, 1995, there was woe and heartache laced in too. Lawrence and Adriana visited midyear, and we were reunited. Great times, and a lot of meeting of the minds for Lawrence and me.

One absolutely bright day in Iquitos on this visit, Lawrence and I were taking lunch at Ari's Burger, the best place in town to eat, with our girlfriends, Adriana and Carmen respectively. We were dominating two tables, a great array of food on one and our planning papers on the other.

It had been a while since they had visited, so we were all happy to see each other and maybe a bit distracted. Normally we watched all our belongings or kept them on our bodies. But hey, we were in Ari's, our lair, and we were protected by his security guard, who was always walking the perimeter of the establishment.

We had our satchels on the document table, and our backpacks were slung over our chairs. We liked the circulating air, and due to Ari's being a corner open-air restaurant, it actually fronted two streets for good cross ventilation. We were seated on the inside edge of one

# CHASING THE DREAM

street sidewalk. The food was great, and we were perusing sketches, calculations, and future building structures for our Yacumama Lodge, 110 miles into the Amazon jungle.

Lawrence was pointing to some details on the plan when he realized that his pack was not slung on the back of his chair any longer.

He looked at me and exclaimed, "My backpack is gone!"

I remembered a well-dressed guy kinda hanging around our tables on the sidewalk. I looked up, and down the street I recognized the pack over the shoulder of the same guy.

I took off out of the restaurant like a bat outa' hell, sprinting down the street after the guy. He saw me coming and started running, which was to no avail, seeing as how I had always taken the blue ribbons home for the fifty- and one-hundred-yard dashes in elementary school.

Needless to say, halfway down the block I tackled him on the sidewalk and threw him in a sleeper hold. Yes, it was Lawrence's pack, with his wallet, passport, money, documents, and all those little personal things that everyone carries in a backpack. I released the sleeper and put him in a hammerlock, waiting for the police to come, which they did.

But it didn't end the way I thought it would. I released the hold, and the guard appeared from Ari's. He looked to be explaining the situation to the police officers. Great, I thought, all right. They motioned for me to take the pack and leave. Okay, I grabbed it and started back up the block with Ari's guard. I looked back over my shoulder. The thief was being placed in the back of the police car and the police drove away. Hmph!

When I got back, scuffed knee and all, Juan, our go-to-guy/translator, told me that the thief would be slapped around a bit and then probably let go. That's it. So we went back to looking at papers, and the girls ate; all was back to normal. Thievery was, and still is, a profession in Iquitos, but that would never happen again to me (Ha!).

We returned to our third-floor loft on Arica Street, and I left to continue my weekly purchases for the lodge. It was May, and the CET groups were to start in a month. We were stoked. The first group was to be twenty-eight guests. Wow…and a few more groups in line until August. We were stylin'.

Carmen and I were both absent from the house for an afternoon later on. Lawrence and Adriana were alone napping. From what I could understand, Carmen came home, and Adriana was in a tizzy. Someone had knocked on our door (they were up and about by now), so Lawrence went down to answer it. When he opened the door, two men showed him their badges: *Seguridad de Estado* (State Security). They proceeded to ask for his papers and passport. They perused them and told him that he had to come with them to answer questions.

Now, mind you, Lawrence did not speak fluent Spanish, and Adriana only spoke Portuguese and a smattering of English. The men's message was clear that Lawrence had to go with them. Period. He gathered his stuff and left with them in a dark sedan.

Carmen sent Pablo after me, and he caught me buying bananas in the mercado. When I arrived at the house, heard the story, and was thinking of how I would be able to find him, Adriana gave me a business card left by the two men. Yup, Seguridad de Estado! There was an address and a telephone number. I called the number and stumbled through my questions. Yes, he was there. I searched and found Juan, and this is what we found: a nondescript building with lettering on the door, *SEGURIDAD DE ESTADO*.

I had perfect papers the whole time I was in Peru, so I could give them a bit of shit. I asked what they were doing, why they had taken my partner into custody. No, he was not in custody; they were only questioning him. Questioning him for what?

## CHASING THE DREAM

English:

"He is here illegally, doing business without the proper visa. We must find out why."

"I want to see him right now, and I want to know what you think he is doing. I manage this company legally, and he and his friend are here visiting us," I parried.

They looked at me for a few moments, then got up from their chairs, saying nothing, entered a room across the hall, and shut the door. I sat there for ten minutes.

The door opened again, and Lawrence was led out between the two men.

"I want privacy," I said.

They led us to a room with a door. I closed it, and we sat down. He looked a bit frazzled and said that they kept asking him the same questions over and over: Why was he here? Did he have money with him? Was he doing business? What was his relationship with me, and would he like to leave (and other stupid questions)?

They had nothing on him; I knew it was a setup to get money. It ended up, after a couple of hours, that they would let him go for a set amount of money. Lawrence had a few powerful new acquaintances in Lima, and we called one in particular. We recounted all that had transpired, and he said that he'd take care of it.

I heard their phone ring and knew it was our mystery man about to kick ass! There was a lot of loud talking, and they hung the phone up with a slam. They opened the door and had Lawrence's jacket, passport, and wallet in hand. The two of them stood at the doorway, and the biggest one said, "*Te puedes ir. Estaremos observandote!*" (You are free to go. We will be watching you.)

What a day. Stressed out and paranoid, we all went out to eat at the Moloka restaurant, trying to make sense of the day.

The next that we heard was that it was an extortion attempt set up by the guard at Ari's (also a policeman), thinking that they could get $10,000 from Lawrence. Aha. "Curses, foiled again!" The guard and the two state security guys were transferred to the frontier with Ecuador for an undisclosed period of time. Lawrence and Adriana were long gone by then. It pays to know the right people.

• • •

The summer passed wonderfully for me, with the CET groups, the influx of money (though of course the groups cost a lot of money to entertain, feed, and move around), and the feeling that we were finally doing something good for the world. When the end of summer arrived we began with FITs (you know, the free independent travelers I talked about), and we made it ready for the October/November group of RHP. We were sailing and into a regimen that really worked.

And then the shit hit the fan and it all came crashing down around me. I still had to keep everything together, because nothing stopped. Guests kept arriving.

One morning in my third-floor office, I was reconciling my checkbook with the monthly statement, and it didn't jibe. It said that I had spent $45,000 more than the checks I had written. I always reconciled at the end of the month with the statement, and I was always dead on and to the dollar. I went to the bank and tried to talk to my agent (whom I had run a ton of money through), but he wasn't there. I asked for another agent to talk to, and they gave me one who was not too cooperative. WTF was going on? He told me that I had written checks in the last month to equal the deductions—but from a different checkbook.

"Listen well, Mr. Bankman. I have no other checkbooks, only this

# CHASING THE DREAM

one. I want to see the checks, my signature, and the date that you say I ordered another checkbook. NOW!"

"That will not be a problem, sir," he said, getting up and walking toward the secretaries in charge of the filing cabinets.

I sat there and fiddled around for a while. Then he returned, saying that I would have to come back in the afternoon.

"I don't think so. I want to talk to your *jefe* (boss), now!"

He was turning paler by the moment. He called the jefe and turned away to say a few words into the phone. I was not getting a good feeling about these actions.

The boss man came out and asked me to step into his office.

"I have reviewed the transactions in your checkbooks, and everything looks fine. You cashed checks totaling $65,000 last month."

"See," I said, "that is the problem. I only have one checkbook that I write checks on, and my checks total about $20,000."

"Oh, well, you ordered a second checkbook. It shows right here," and he showed me a document that was unrecognizable to me and a signature that was nothing at all like mine.

I began by saying, "Your bank (by the way, it was the *Banco de Credito*, common throughout Peru, the second-most-influential power next to the president of the nation) has cashed at least seventy-five of my checks. They always check my signature and my identification. I never go to a teller; I have an official agent here who gets my money and delivers it to my hand. You know that. How can one of your agents give out $45,000 to someone, not me, in a thirty-day period, and not check identification? Show me the checks. I want to see the signature."

He told me to wait while he searched for the documents. He left the room, and I began to put the puzzle together: It had to be my accountant. He did not have access to my checkbook, but he knew everyone in the bank. I remembered the first time I walked into the Banco de Credito with him. All of the *funcionarios* (official agents) waved, shook his hand, said *hola*, or nodded at him as we walked by.

He was recommended to me by Dr. Teddy, who was our lawyer, remember? So now we had one of the most renowned lawyers and one of the most renowned accountants in Iquitos. I was starting to wonder if it was renowned or infamous.

The jefe opened the door, walked over to his desk, and sat down with no documents in his hand. That was a little strange since he left to locate them.

"You will have to contact our legal department now, for I have been advised that they will take care of your dispute."

GOODBYE...

The rest of this occurrence was a train wreck for us, so I will breeze through it so as not to drag you any further into the mire of a "banana republic versus gringos" (which I ran into five times in my years there).

Here goes: It appeared that at least six funcionarios were involved in the fraud. Our accountant ordered a new checkbook starting at 001 (I was already at 085 in my original) with my trusted official agent. This order had to go through quite a few agents to spit out a new checkbook, and it did. Everyone got a piece of the action.

I took legal action against poor Alejandro, my accountant, who professed his innocence and then admitted to the whole scam. I filed a complaint; he was picked up, placed in jail, and admitted that he had done the deed! I began investigating and discovered that he had applied for a license to conduct business as a discotheque owner. I acquired the address and found his wife there running the place. We confiscated whatever we could and recouped maybe $3,000. I never discovered the location of the rest of the money. Alejandro was released from jail

## CHASING THE DREAM

(don't ask me how) escaped to Lima, and died there from a massive stroke and heart attack.

Funny thing, though, his wife was very well dressed and had a new lover. Go figure!

We brought in a lawyer from a Lima firm to pursue a suit against Banco de Credito. We went to court, and our case was dismissed—no fault for BdeC. I also found out that the law firm also represented Banco de Credito, and the judge threw it out for "conflict of interests." I guess it was planned. Iquitos is a jungle city, and word had it that seven funcionarios were fired two days after the trial.

To add insult to injury, BdeC sued us for default on our account, and froze thousands of dollars that we had in another bank. They won and took our money. That ended as: Lawrence and Norman sporting very unhappy faces.

I still had to run a business, and we still had tourists arriving, so "the show must go on." It did! (Thank you, Freddy.)

# TEN

**I WILL TELL YOU,** after living through this year with all the ups and downs, joys and pains, I decided to take a family vacation. We were planning to start at the top of Peru, in Tumbes, and work our way down along the beaches to Ica. We really needed the ocean. We had come to Los Congrejos before, near Piura, to spend a week with Carmen's sister Claudeth and her family. We rented a beachfront condo and just sat in the sand and swam in the ocean.

One time we brought Carmen's mom, Olga, with all the kids. It was one of the best times we had ever had. Even Tia Juana came to Piura to see us. Beach time was great and a big change from the jungle.

This time I wanted to decompress. Was there a better way to let it all go than to be on the beach with the ocean breeze brushing the stress from my fiber? I don't think so.

We did start in Tumbes, a stinky, stinky city. It is a fishing port, but a little bit over the top. We spent one night there, and in the morning started our road trip down the Pacific coast of Peru. I hired a car to take us to Zorritos, where there was a nice resort. I wanted to read, sculpt, play in the sand and water, and eat good food. It was all good,

## CHASING THE DREAM

and I actually finished a sculpture and a drawing there. In the hotel restaurant, on the way to bathroom, there was a small waiting room. In that room was a bamboo and thatch chair that I fell in love with and wanted to make immortal. This is the black and white version:

*Bamboo chair, Zorritos, Peru*

We stayed at the Zorritos resort for a week, and I sat in front of the room working on a native sculpture all week. It was carved from cumaceba wood, very hard, and medicinal in resin form as well as tea. All the raw materials were obtained in the jungle and on the beach. I just put them all together.

*Minimalistic Amazon Chieftain*

We continued down the Pan-American Highway until we reached Punta Sal. The taxi driver told us that it was the best resort on the coast. Guess what? It was! We bought the all-inclusive package which included very good meals, some excursions, and great music. We were introduced to the music of Laura Pausini on this trip and fell in love with her. I still have her original CDs that we bought in 1996, and we still play them.

Nayla struck up a friendship with a Russian girl, and we had the most spacious bungalow at the resort. There was a small *palapa* in front of our bungalow, and with the setting sun we were in paradise. The most daring thing that we tried was the new parasailing. Strapped

## CHASING THE DREAM

into a parachute, hooked to a speedboat, and pulled up into the air, we were able to view the world from 100-plus feet above the earth. It was pretty cool.

So we were in our second week, and I was not accustomed to having this much time not working. FREE! I bit the bullet, though, and we took off for Ica. We skirted around Lima and arrived in the desert. The Nazca Lines were there, and an incredible resort created by the same guy who extracted Lawrence from the Seguridad de Estado in Iquitos.

The weather and the pool were so nice that we played around for hours. When we went back to the room I felt a bit tingly, and noticed that we all looked kind of pink. After showering and realizing that we had stayed in the sun too long, we took a cab into the town to eat. It was a nonconsequential meal, nothing to remember—until later, when we all got sick.

I knew that we were going to be very uncomfortable trying to sleep, and remembered that Carmen's dad, Don Teddy, had told me that Kolynos toothpaste eased the pain of sunburn. We stopped and bought a couple of tubes and struggled back to the hotel room, applied the toothpaste to our sizzling skin and tried to sleep.

Middle of the night is when the sickness hit us. Oh boy, must have been something we ate, LOL. We staggered back to Lima and then Iquitos, wondering when all would be well again. Vacation was over and time to put my nose to the grindstone. You know, I can't believe that my nose has gotten so big, when I have been grinding it away for all these years.

PART 8
# CALIFORNIA AND BEYOND
*1970-1971*

# ELEVEN

**WE REALLY HAD OUR WORK** cut out for us. Spring was introducing itself little by little, and that was a godsend. We had weathered a very cold and rainy Northern California winter in a tent with a space heater (good thing that was way in the past).

Now that we were in the sheep shed and summer was raising its head, life was easier. We did do things, of course. Larry read an esoteric book collection on magic and manifestations. I wrote songs; one that I remember, "High Hill Wind," was written about the wind that flowed down the hill behind our tent. *"Here it comes again, in a high hill wind. Words I sing are whispered through your hair."* I was referring to the tall-bending grass on the hillside.

I dabbled in making a bit of gold and silver jewelry, which was why Thayer had me make that belt buckle for her boyfriend. And we had to get Nicky to school, of course. Thayer and her boyfriend came out often, and they had a renovated tool shed for their lair.

I played my songs in the area's coffee shops and inns. There were quite a few, so I was able to perform at least once a week. Uncle Sam's in Mill Valley and The Inn of the Beginning in Cotati were my favorites. At this time all the coffee shops and inns with live music were like Old English establishments: kind of dark, and some were smoky, with hippies, bohemians, and even some old beatniks. It was wonderful because everyone listened to the music.

Like I mentioned earlier, we had good organic food, a place to live-work-sleep, solitude, and all the "mind refreshments" we wanted. Life just ambled on for months: us making the sheep shed an okay place to live, Thayer and her man visiting the ranch (as they called it) with a few of his partners to play loud raucous electric music until the wee hours of the morning.

Then one day we got a call from two old friends: my "brutha from anotha mutha," Jim, and Roger. That was cool because we were good friends from Goshen, and they were on their way somewhere. I remember that the best thing about the ranch for Jim was the glass shower, but he was always worried about the cows and the horses seeing his service revolver. We had a bunch of good times, and then they went on their way up to Washougal, Washington.

Winter was rapidly approaching again, and we were getting ready for the cold. We had a wood-burning stove, so wood had to be purchased and gathered; we weather-proofed the windows with thick clear plastic, bought back-up food for Sunshine (Thayer's Harlequin Great Dane), and stuck newspaper into all the cracks in the walls. After all, it was a sheep shed.

We had a real telephone sitting on an end table. It hardly ever rang, but that day it did, and it was Larry's brother, John. What a gas. The last time I had seen John was at the Oxbow Park in Goshen, Indiana. Larry, John, and I had snuck into the park after closing time (like 10:00 p.m.) and built a fire, took some crazy medicine, and began playing our music. I was on guitar, Larry on harmonica, and John on drum. We were jammin', baby!

## CHASING THE DREAM

In that time and place, we were legends in our own minds—"outstanding in our fields." Literally! But we were having the times of our lives and going full throttle...then we saw the sheriff's truck pull into the park. It had to happen.

"Hey, guys, just act like we belong here," I said. "All we are doing is playing music."

The truck wound around the entrance and stopped about twenty feet from us. No siren, no lights; he knew there was no danger.

Of course, our eyes had to look like pinwheels and everything was reverberating and tracing, but we were just three normal Goshen guys out for the evening in a prohibited area. The officer got out of his truck, hitched up his service belt, and walked toward us.

"Hey, guys, what are you doing here at this hour? The park is closed."

John, I believe, was working at the park at that time—he had keys to get in. He turned and whispered, "That's Terry."

So I said, "Hey, Terry, how are you? You know how hard it is to find a place to just sit and talk, play some music, and not be bothered."

"Yeah, but you started a fire, and I got a call."

"Well, you are here now, and nothing is going on. Hey, we have an extra drum. You want to jam with us?"

He was surprised at first, then totally stoked and ready to participate. He accepted the drum, and I started playing a random riff. John and Larry joined in, and then he did too. Believe it or not, he had rhythm. He kept up and became one of the gang. We played for hours, and when the bonfire finally became embers and we were laughing and jawing about nonsensical topics, we decided that it was time to call it quits. We doused the fire, started walking toward the road, and Terry offered us a ride over to Larry's parents' house.

What a guy...what a complete "officer of the law." We never spent any more time with him, but when I saw him on his patrols he always waved, as I did in return.

Sorry for the diversion, but that was important to me. I'll get right back to the story now.

John told us that in a couple of weeks he was coming to see us at the ranch. Well, that was great because Larry and I were getting a touch of cabin fever in our blood. Alone in the dismal California winter, without any sun for about three weeks, cold drizzle every day—I would say we needed some new energy at the old Frog Holler!

It was just like old times, some of this and some of that; John on drum, Larry on harmonica, and me on the new Martin D-35. We made a lot of progress on nothing and achieved more and more unity, but it was a bit redundant at times.

I had been talking about going to visit Missy (an old friend) somewhere up in Northern California at a commune called Fat City. Someone had to stay at the ranch; John was interested in going, so that cinched it.

Thayer's man had that brother, and he had a VW Bus that we were using at the ranch for transportation, so Larry bought a bunch of supplies for his week at the ranch with no vehicle. John and I packed up the bus for our week on the road, said our see-ya-laters, and headed up north.

We were planning on sleeping in the V-dub, so we brought our down-fart-bags, warm clothes, and hippy-kibble (granola) for the trip. We always had the proverbial gallon of non-filtered organic apple juice and water, so we were stylin'.

The VW was great for snowy roads because the engine, and hence all the weight, was in the back of the vehicle. We were going along, snow in the air, snow on the road, and nothing in our minds. By the time we reached Red Bluff, we were on a roll. We only had another 127 miles to go, and we could do that in about two and a half hours. It was late in the day, and I wondered if we should stop in a small town and sleep for the night.

Well, I decided to go on up to Redding, but about three miles before Anderson I started to hear a strange sound from the rear of the bus. Now, everything is amplified in the back of an empty VW Bus. This was a bad sound, though. Like gears grinding. The Anderson exit appeared; I turned to look at John.

"I think we should pull in here to see what is happening with the rear end."

"Good idea," said John.

Of course it was Saturday night, and it was starting to get dark. I exited and headed toward Anderson, California, just a mile inland. There was one service station open, but it looked as though he was closing as I drove up. I got out and entered the office.

"Good evening, I am about ready to close for the night," a big lumberjack-type guy said. "I'll be open tomorrow after church."

"We are on our way to Yreka, and there is a problem with the rear end," I told him. "Are you a mechanic?"

"Yes I am, but I am going home now. You will have to wait until tomorrow."

"Could you just listen to it, and see if we can go on to Yreka or not?" I asked.

"Okay, start her up, and try to go forward and then reverse."

I did as he said, knowing already that the transaxle was going out. I shifted into first and advanced ten feet. *Grind—grind.* I braked, shifted into reverse, and moved a few feet. *Grind—grind—grind!* Not a good sound.

"That is your transaxle, buddy. No good."

"I figured as much. Can I fix it tomorrow? Are there parts here?" I asked.

We introduced ourselves. He was Will. We shook hands, and I explained our situation. He told me that he couldn't do anything that night, but we could sleep in our bus inside his garage, and he would try to get us back on the road after church. Nobody could ask for more than that. He advised me that we would be locked in, though. No problem; we had empty water containers in the bus, LOL!

It was a tough night; the temperature dipped to about thirty degrees. It was a good thing that we were inside his garage. Down bags are warm, and we made it through the night. Our water had ice in it in the morning, and all our bodily movements were sloth-like, but we were up and ready to go.

Will showed up at around 10:00 in the morning—after church—telling me that he had a friend who owned a salvage yard. We could go to the yard and dismantle an old VW Bus for the transaxle. His friend would charge me $150 for it, and if I did the work there would be no other charges. Much better than a poke in the eye, wouldn't you say?

Most VW repairs were relatively simple if you kept all the nuts and bolts together and didn't mix things up. The transaxle was out in an hour, and we transported it back to the garage in the back of Will's pickup, my fingers frozen.

Just to explain what a transaxle is: It is a very large conglomeration of metal parts. It takes at least two to three men to pick it up. I had jacks under it to unbolt it from the motor, but when it was free I had to balance it on a floor jack to slide it out from under the old bus. We did it, and then the second chapter began: installation of the transaxle. You know that I had to dismantle the old one before I could install the new/used one, right?

## **CHASING THE DREAM**

I did it in a little less than an hour; the garage was a bit warmer than outside, so it went faster. To install it, the driving shaft had to be at the exact angle with the motor so the teeth line up and the shaft could slide into the motor. Hmmm, that sounds familiar on a lot of levels, doesn't it?

This process took two or three tries. When we had it fitted and ready to bolt in, I let out a breath and finished up the job. Lordy be, if it weren't for people like Will and his friend Bobby, we would have been stranded on I-5 in the night. God bless them, and I just pray that I always help anyone in need of a hand. Amen.

I paid Bobby and offered Will money, but he looked at me like I was crazy and told me that he didn't do anything, that I had done all the work. By the way, he lent me all his tools to do the job. *Two days ago I couldn't even spell mechanic, and now I am one!* I thought.

Sunday, 2:00 p.m., we were entering I-5 on our way to see Missy. 4:45 p.m., we were pulling into Fat City exhausted but content. "Hi Missy, how you been?"

We hung for a few days, checking the place out. I had thoughts of possibly asking to be accepted into the fold, but it really wasn't for me. The thing that I remember the most, other than the rams in rut, was the salmon tooth that Missy gave me to thread onto my gold earring. I was cool. Back down I-5 traveled John and I. Hi-ho, hi-ho, it's back to the ranch we go.

# TWELVE

**FROG HOLLER WAS VERY COZY** compared to what we had just experienced on our road trip. My peeled knuckles from the transaxle exchange were healing nicely, and we were settling back into the groove.

One evening, Sunshine, the Great Dane whom Thayer had bred with another Harlequin, sounded like she was about to give birth. I called Thayer and alerted her, knowing she would want to be with us. She arrived about an hour later, and Sunshine was in the process. She gave birth to five pups and was taking care of them. They were suckling and acting like pups, but Sunshine acted weird.

Thayer left the next day, and we were with the five new kids. Sunshine acted like she was worried about something, and because she had been living in the same house with me I picked up on it. She seemed to get weirder and weirder, until I decided to check her out. She was nursing her pups, and I heard her whimpering. I advanced on her and tried to comfort her, but she would have nothing to do with me. She looked like she was in pain, and I decided to see if she had a problem with her privates. OMG, there was a little paw sticking out of her vagina.

## CHASING THE DREAM

There was a dead pup inside of her. They hadn't all been deported. I tried to pet her, but her eyes were in pain, and I knew that if the pup didn't leave, she would get a massive infection and die.

I decided that there was only one action to take. I had to get that pup out of her.

A Harlequin Great Dane is a very large dog, but not like a cow or a horse. The birth canal was limited in size, but it had to be extracted. This was a very difficult thing to do, but I did it. I carefully stuck my fingers into her opening, grabbed the little legs, and slowly pulled the dead pup out. She whimpered through the whole process, but relaxed when it was finished. A very bad smell followed, and she tried to get to the dead pup. I let her sniff it in my hand, and then retreated to the kitchen to get a bag to place it in. Maybe that was a mistake, I do not know.

I called Thayer and relayed all of the information. I advised her that I should pack Sunshine up and take her to the vet immediately. Thayer would meet me there. It was quite a process because she had five live pups, and she had to take care of them, but Sunshine's life was at stake. Did we really have to feed the pups until the mom returned? I guess so.

Luckily she was only gone for a day and a half, and her milk did not dry up. Back in the sheep shed she was mom again, and the little sucklings were as happy as pigs in shit. Mom had been shot up with antibiotics, cleaned out, and washed up. Ready to be mom again.

There was only one residual problem: Sunshine never liked me after this issue. I was not used to that because all animals loved me, loved to be around me, and wanted to be by my side. She actually growled at me and avoided me. I guess she might have blamed me for her stillborn baby. Oh well, life goes on; sunshine is gone, I am old, and all has passed on.

## NORMAN WALTERS

• • •

Spring had sprung. John was long gone, and I was collecting miner's lettuce, shepherd's purse, and a few mushrooms for our dietary needs. Life was good, and we had made a connection with the Ananda Marga ashram in Sonoma. Some old friends from the New York days who were involved in the ashram connected with us, and I began backing up and accompanying the wife, Uma, in a duo called "Norman and Uma."

We played the Circle Star Theatre south of San Francisco and a few other venues, and later dissolved into the forgotten world of West Coast musical groups.

One night when the "big boys" were at the ranch playing their loud discordant music—loaded beyond the word—I felt the need to write a song. There was an old '55 Plymouth or Desoto (I can't remember which) sitting at the top of the property by the leaking pond (where there were tons of frogs, hence the name Frog Holler).

I crawled into the backseat with my D-35 and tried to focus through the haze of a heaping teaspoon of psilocybin. For some unearthly reason my guitar and that powder blended together like a match made in Heaven (if there is such a place), and I began playing. It is probably one of the weirdest songs I have ever written, but the most fun to play. There were different sized "camel bells" hanging from the rearview mirror, and it gave me an idea for the name of the song: "Sons of the Desert."

I tied the bells to my right foot and stomped on the downbeat. Man, I was in the hot dusty desert, riding a camel. Maybe not, but inspiration was running wild.

The next thing I knew, the front door opened; I had visitors, Larry and Uma, trying to escape from the volume 10 music below. It was cool; it didn't bother me. I just continued on my voyage to the

# CHASING THE DREAM

unknown. It appeared that we were all in the same boat, LOL, because not a word was spoken.

I had a sketchbook open, with an HB drawing pencil, and I was trying to catch the lyrics as they danced across the page. I guess I was catching more than lyrics, because when I got the book into the light, there was a drawing interlacing the words.

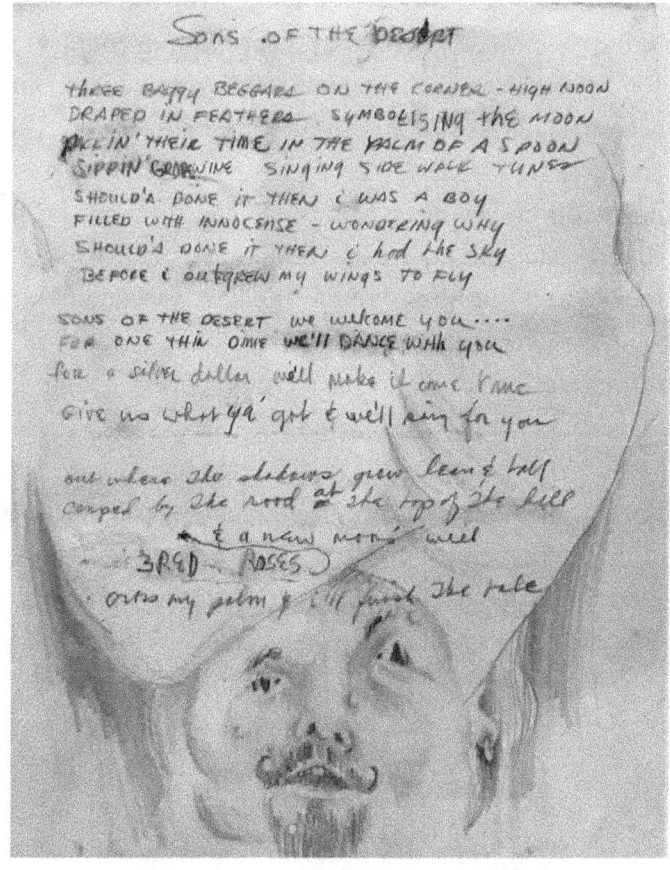

*Sons of the Desert, N. Walters 1971*

## NORMAN WALTERS

• • •

When all of these incredible experiences were subsiding and finally became stagnant (like always), Larry and I came up with a new idea: ride horses to the East Coast, buy some land, and be back-to-the-land-ers! I was reading a book about John Muir, adventurer extraordinaire, and his trail up the Pacific Coast. Wouldn't it be great?

We'd buy horses, supplies, chart the route (up John's trail, across Canada, down the Appalachian Trail), buy land in the mountains, build log cabins, and grow our own food. Man, that would be the life, wouldn't it (in 1971)?

Well, it was March when we started this. We did buy the horses and all the tack. We made our buckskin clothing. We made lists and checked them twice. We rode our horses on the Dolcinis' farmland (with permission, of course) and had a blast. Two Indiana boys gone wild.

The time drew nearer, and we were preparing for the inevitable. Then the "wet kiss…at the end of the hot fist" came again. My horse, a beautiful Arabian/Quarter mix (a gelding, black, with three white stockings and a blaze—older, but in good shape), decided to throw a wrench in the works. Larry and I had just returned from a great ride over hill and dale, and we were coming upon the stable when the old boy reared—bucked—and threw me. I landed well and got up (mind you, I was raised with some horses, and I knew how to ride), and saw him facing me off about twenty feet away.

Hmm, that was a strange thing to have happen this late in the game. I stood looking at him, focusing all my energy. He pawed the ground like a bull in Madrid. I never said a word but looked into his eyes and sent out the message, "Come to me!"

## **CHASING THE DREAM**

He looked up from under his brows, staring at me. I stared back, and kept sending out the message, "Come to me!"

He snorted a few times, looked to the side, and took a few steps toward me. I continued (mentally) giving the command, and slowly, shaking his head and pawing the ground, he arrived in front of me. I held my hand out, and he brought his head up and nuzzled my hand. I wrapped my arms around his neck and hugged him.

I understood what he was telling me: "I am too old and cannot do what you are asking of me. I want to be free and finish my life in peace." I didn't know he was retirement age.

Well, that really added a new tile to our domino game. What would we do? It was May and we had to get moving. By June, it would be too late, and we would be caught in the snow.

• • •

**A NEW GAME PLAN:** Okay, Larry and I had always been able to turn the tides of woe into success, and I was hoping our luck would hold. We would sell the horses and tack, figure out a way to get to the East Coast, and end up with the same finale that we had planned: Back to the Land.

We could do it; I knew we could.

I had been seeing Rita for a couple of months. She worked in the juice bar at the natural food store (the Grainery) across the street from the Inn of the Beginning in Cotati. She was happy when I told her that we were not riding horses to the East Coast, but unhappy when I mentioned that we were searching for a way to eventually culminate our plan.

One beautiful June day, we made a trip to Cotati to buy some food. Walking into the Grainery, I noticed that Rita's smile was exceptional—she was happy about something. It was good to see after days of stagnation at the ranch. We had finally made the decision to buy a van and drive east until we found our destination. We believed that we were putting the puzzle pieces in the right places.

Rita took a break, and the three of us went outside for a walk and talk. The Great Spirit then changed the course of our lives.

"I have a car, and I want to go with you!" she exclaimed.

Well gosh, that really came out of left field. Rita was a New York Jewish girl. She had never camped, never been in the wilderness, never gathered wild things for eating or endured nature's hardships (sometimes very cruel)—but she was beaming.

"I want to go. I want to try to be courageous, on the edge, like you two, and live a different kind of life. I have always been safe, and I have never taken a shot in the dark."

I guess we were the "dark" she wanted to take a shot at. This was a hard decision for me. I mean, we weren't committed to each other; we were very casual, but had spent time together. She had a good, wry sense of humor, a Brooklyn accent, and a wild side, I guess.

Larry and I did our eye communications, gestures, and mumblings, and I shrugged my shoulders…and so did he. I mean, she had a car, she had the nerve (it appeared), she was cool and unattached (maybe).

Okay, so we made a deal. Larry and I would pay for all the gas and car repairs (if there were any); we would go thirds on the land; and we would be pioneers together. Sounds good, right? *"The best-laid plans of mice and men…"* Robert Burns had something to say about that.

## PART 9
# GROUPS, GROUPS, AND THE FISHING MAFIA

*Yacumama Lodge*
*Rio Yarapa*
*1995-1999*

# THIRTEEN

**HERE WE ARE AGAIN,** out on the lazy (ten-knot current) Yarapa River. We were pretty well settled into this area. All I really had to think about was keeping things together, and in our off-season time, building what was needed for the group-size growth each year. For our first three-and-a-half-month high season, beginning in June, I figured I would have to build five more bungalows and another dual bathroom.

The other new addition would be a laundry area with rainwater collection and pumped river water when necessary. We had sent a buttload of tools and articles from the USA in 1992, and we had included two hand washing machines with wringers. The only thing missing now was the ability to *dry* the clothes. This was a very big deal when you were talking *sweating tourists.*

We kicked around some ideas of how big, how to generate the heat, how to control the heat, and how to make it safe. I designed a wood-burning stove that was fed from the outside of the building with an eight-inch smokestack through the ceiling. We decided on the dimensions and lined the inside walls and ceiling with galvanized sheet metal to reflect and contain the heat.

I drew the plans for the stove, took them to my favorite welder, gave him my requirements for steel thickness, and he told me that it would be ready when I came back from the jungle on Friday. As I was walking out the door, I thought of something else that I wanted. May as well kill two birds (even though I didn't want to kill any birds) with one stone, so I went back into his shop. I explained to him what I wanted for the lodge kitchen: two, one-quarter-inch-thick steel griddles (for pancakes, eggs, and the likes), but I wanted him to heat and bend all four sides up about one centimeter and add a handle on each end (they were rectangles) for carrying. He looked at me like he always did, "crazy gringo," and said he'd try. I still have one twenty-four years later, and we still use it.

I needed some fire clay for where the stove passed through the wooden wall. I contacted my *ferreteria* (hardware store) friend Roger, whose family owned a brick factory. He didn't carry refractory clay, heat-resistant mortar, and didn't know where to find it. His brother brought me what they use: *flor de arena,* the first two to four inches of clay right under the layer of fallen leaves deep in the jungle. He brought me three *costales* (rice bags) full of the stuff. I bought a bunch of their bricks, thanked them, and merrily went my way.

There were a lot of imagined calculations, like how hot is this room really going to get? How much wood to stuff in the hopper? How close can the clothing and sheets be in proximity to the stove? These were the unknowns. I took my best shot at it, and it came out really well. I tightly strung galvanized wire around the top, wall-to-wall with forked-hardwood sticks, to minimize sag just like my mom did in the 1950s on our clothesline.

Well, I'll tell ya, we done good! I set the stove, bricked the opening, mortared it in with my clay (which hardened when heated), and we were ready for a test. The miracle "dry house" was about thirteen feet by

## CHASING THE DREAM

fifteen feet by seven feet high, maybe a little more; I left space around the stove so nothing would burn up. The stove was about a meter long. For it to work, the wood had to be stacked correctly so as not to make hot spots in the metal. The workers never got the hang of it, so we had hot spots.

Stack it up with wood, hang up some different types of clothes, and see what we got. We got good news:

Sheets dry in twenty-five minutes, T-shirts and long-sleeve shirts in thirty minutes, blankets and tourist pants in forty to forty-five minutes, and blue jeans in one hour. In-frikkin-credible.

We were going to have some stylin' guests. No more stinky tourists. It did get ripe sometimes. Some of the administrators and instructors from the groups who came various times year after year told me, "You don't want customs looking through your bag? Put your stinky underwear and socks right on top." LOL.

Sooo…by the time our first group of CET arrived, I had those bungalows built, the wash and dry house working, and the dual bathroom flushing too. We were ready to receive. I even installed a UHF communication radio system, made possible by the solar electric system we'd installed the year before. That was imperative. Being linked to the Iquitos office saved us from disaster quite a few times.

• • •

We finished out a very successful season, with thumbs-up from CET and RHP. The latter's first groups were the beginning of a quest to find the correct way to aid the forgotten people of the Amazon, which they did.

Patty and Sadie, co-founders of Rainforest Health Project, introduced doctors, nurses, medical students, and lay volunteers to the joys and sorrows associated with caring and giving of themselves.

They were able to conduct physicals, treat wounds, diagnose illnesses, perform small surgical procedures, deliver babies, and create permanent records for everyone they saw. The ER was at the lodge, and there were quite a few instances each trip.

Not only did the villagers benefit from their visits, but the volunteers, our employees, and their families did also. One trip in the mid-nineties, there was Mike, a family member of one of the administrators. He was in his late forties and was helping with clerical work: filling out cards, documenting information, and some triaging.

One morning at breakfast, he said that he wasn't feeling well. He didn't eat much, but it seemed to pass, and he went on the daily clinic to Puerto Miguel. While the clinic was being set up, Mike seemed to feel worse. He complained of pain and indigestion and felt weak.

On this particular trip, RHP had a renowned cardiologist along. She became aware of Mike's situation and diagnosed "heart attack." She did have medication and administered it. Mike appeared to feel better, but he was very weak.

She broke the news, "Mike has to go to Iquitos to the hospital! I think that he has had at least two attacks."

We had fast boats, and I sanctioned our good old *Yacuruna* for the trip. It could reach Iquitos in under three hours with just a few people in the boat. They set up a comfortable place for Mike and Sandy, the cardiologist, Sadie (administrator and wife), helpers and the boat captain, and they sped off to Iquitos.

I radioed the office to alert my assistant and prepare transportation. When they arrived, Mike was worse but holding on. He was wired up, IV-tubed, and he had survived a few more small attacks on the way in. *Yacuruna* pulled up to the municipal port and they whisked him away to the hospital, only to encounter disappointment and frustration.

## CHASING THE DREAM

Remember where we were: a jungle city with no roads in from anywhere! Hospitals that were understaffed, not really hygienic, under-supplied, and staff under-trained. The best medical treatment available was at the Clinica Ana Stahl, a Seventh-Day Adventist clinic started by missionaries many years earlier. It was clean, but there was one problem: The doctors had a bit of a chip on their shoulders when it came to advice from an outsider.

This cardiologist, Sandy, who had been treating Mike—keeping him alive—for the last four-plus hours with state-of-the-art technology in her brain from saving people every day in her state-of-the-art hospital in Chicago, told them that there was a drug they could get from the pharmacy that would keep him alive. She used it every day, and it was proven.

The doctor told her that he couldn't administer it because it wasn't an "authorized" heart drug, and he didn't know about it. He could only administer a drug that was known and used in Peru. He would have to remove her IV and introduce a new one administering his recommended drug.

The Chicago heart doc took Sadie aside and said, "If we leave him here, he'll die."

Well, that was all it took for things to start moving. They checked Mike out of the clinic, signed the disclaimer as they were situating him (with the IV) into a motocar, and sped off to the hotel. They checked in, got Mike situated in bed, and Sadie made the call to Medevac Travel Insurance in the USA. This is an insurance that you can buy when you are traveling to a medically questionable country and may have an accident or health problem. The company will send a jet airplane hospital to your location to pick you up, stabilize you, and take you to the closest hospital in the USA.

It was 5:00 in the afternoon, and they informed her that a plane would be landing at the airport in Iquitos, Peru, in the early hours of the next morning. They would update her as to exact time when they had the information. My Iquitos office was updating us at Yacumama Lodge every hour.

Sandy stayed with Mike. Sadie—a registered nurse—ran to the pharmacy with a list of things to buy, and Mike couldn't have been in better hands. They kept up the vigil all night.

The plane arrived in the morning; a fully equipped hospital was behind the door. Mike was flown to the USA and admitted into a hospital. Sadie and Sandy accompanied him all the way. We were informed that Mike was going to live. He'd had eleven heart attacks before Sandy could get him stabilized in the hotel room with the IV drug. His heart was torn up, and he would have to take it easy while he waited for a new heart. He was placed on the list, and from what I heard, he received his new "pumper" and he is alive today. We are friends on Facebook, LOL.

These are the stories and accountings that make our service and our lives worthwhile. There are unbelievable lifesaving events that have happened, from snake bite to machete wounds to shotgun wounds, and almost every emergency you can imagine.

I remember the wife of my friend Pancho being attacked by thousands of bees while paddling her canoe to the Ucayali River in the flood season. These were not honeybees; these were a very aggressive bee that swarmed and attacked, trying to overcome their adversary.

She was just calmly paddling her canoe through the forest when a swarm overtook her. She eventually fell into the water, and they flew away. Another villager witnessed the attack, rescued her from the water, and said that he couldn't even see her face or head for the bees. They brought her to the lodge immediately. She was stung hundreds of times, and the stingers were still sticking out of her face and arms. She was starting to swell, and I knew she would be toxified in a very short period of time.

My speedboat could have her in the Nauta Hospital in less than thirty minutes. Off we went…no time to spare. We had transportation waiting for us and got her into Emergency in forty-five minutes (from the lodge). She had been stung over 500 times; within three hours you could not even tell who she was from the swelling of her face and scalp.

All they could do was IV her and add an antihistamine. In a week she returned to Puerto Miguel, much better but weary. Life is tough in the jungle.

# FOURTEEN

**ONE OF THE GROUPS OF CET,** a group of thirty kids (with eight staff and four PhDs as instructors), was an eye-opener. They were aware, interested in the environment, and worried about the future (this was in 1995). One of the travelers, a boy of fourteen, was very much interested in the future of recycling and new wood cutting around the world (for "thermal copying"). Since we were protecting 7,700 acres of the jungle around Yacumama Lodge, he was my buddy, always interested in anything I had to say about conservation.

The teaching excursions ended in the afternoon around 4:00. That way everyone could relax a bit, shower, and be ready for dinner at 6:00. One evening I had showered and was in my cabin dressing for dinner.

Don Teddy, my father-in-law, called out to me, "Sr. Norman, there is a problem in the main bathroom."

I followed him to the building. We entered the empty girls' side, and one of the two lavatories was lying on the floor, cracked. There was water all over because the inlet hoses had broken when the sink fell, draining the elevated water tank.

"What happened?" I asked.

## CHASING THE DREAM

"I really don't know," he said. "I heard the water dripping through the floorboards and came to investigate."

We didn't have an extra lavatory, so we just cleaned it up and shut off the water inlet for the sink. I was thinking that I would address the problem after dinner when we were all gathered.

We had a great dinner of grilled fish, rice and beans, steamed vegetables, tomato and cucumber salad, with flan for dessert. Everyone loved the dinner, as always, and when all the plates were cleared away it was time for the "after dinner discussion" they had every evening before the night excursions (caiman hunting, jungle walk, etc.).

I decided to start it out, and asked them all if anyone knew how the girls' bathroom lavatory ended up on the floor. Nobody seemed to know anything, so I advised the administrators and chaperones to find out and let me know who was responsible, and they would have to pay for the sink.

That night before bed, Jim (one of the organizers) came to me and said, "We found out who was in the bathroom and talked to them. They explained that the mirrors were hung a little bit high, and they couldn't see themselves, so they barely leaned against the lavatory, on tiptoes, and it came crashing to the floor. They had been very scared and ran to their shared room." Jim told me that they wanted to write letters to me apologizing for the incident.

In the morning before breakfast, I was sitting at a table drinking my coffee as always, and two young girls asked to talk to me. They looked pretty scared, and they both handed me notes.

These two girls from Noblesville, Indiana—my home state, a very favorite group—were the same age and were always together in the meetings and excursions. They were attentive, on time, and displayed interest in all classes. Good young folk. I read the notes; they were very apologetic and understanding about how hard I had worked to build this lodge.

I still have the notes, and as a matter of fact, I had to read them again to jog my memory. Sweethearts, both of them. I had a new sink installed before the next group arrived, making sure that I installed it on the wall with through-bolts this time.

One year, I believe it was 1995, at the end of our season when the groups were finished and all we had booked were FITs, an RHP group in October, and a GreenTracks group (aha, you haven't heard of this booking agency yet, have you?) over New Year's Eve, it was looking like a high-water year was coming on.

GreenTracks was best known (to us) for Bill's herpetology tours (amphibians and reptiles)—I am talking SNAKES and other crawling, swimming, biting, and gnawing things. I love them, but I know that they do scare some people.

We had already hosted the Smithsonian's Entomology (insects) Laboratory (U.S. National Museum of Natural History, Washington, D.C.). Dave and Jim headed up the group, finding and studying unbelievable insects. Jim even discovered a new type of katydid while he was with us. Dave had clearance to take some specimens back (alive) for the Smithsonian Insect Zoo. They were with us for two weeks. That was an eye-opening experience!

I can't forget Peruvian ornithologist Thomas Valqui, who wrote the first Peruvian book of birds. He visited for a couple of weeks, sighting, hearing, and finding traces of an incredible number of species, and over 600 different birds.

He told me that a paradise tanager could only be viewed with binoculars because they lived in the upper canopy of the rainforest. Boy oh boy, that gave me the second signal whispering in my ear, "Build a tower!" Remember the first? Lawrence and I were up on the Cumaceba Creek when I climbed a large banyan tree. Seeing above the understory was enough for me to say, "I want to see over the jungle all the way to Brazil."

## CHASING THE DREAM

Very soon, everyone who visited Yacumama Lodge would have the opportunity to touch angel wings in the jungle.

• • •

I was able to spend a bit of time with my Peruvian family in the off season. I always went to the lodge when there were guests, but the vacant weeks were for my recharging.

I received a call from the DL (remember her?) in Iquitos, advising me that she was traveling to the village of Jaldar, very close to *Uvos Cocha* (Lake Uvos), to cut the fishermen's nets. They were killing pink dolphins that got tangled up in the nets, attempting to eat the trapped fish. She was paying the Forest Police to go with her. Did I want to go? She could take photos of us for her American newsletter, and it would be great for Yacumama promotion.

"Whoa!" I exclaimed. "What are you thinking? We are trying to leave the smallest footprint possible, to not be the 'ugly Americans' in the eyes of the villagers. Sure, the fishermen are doing a horrible thing, and they are netting the mouth of the lake for commercial gain, but do you really want your face on the front of a 'Wanted' poster? Why not have the police just roll up the nets so the pinks can escape? They could leave advisories for the fishermen."

"No, that would never work. We have to teach them," she said.

"Well, have a fun time, but be careful. Uvos is a deep lake, and there are not many people around, just fishermen. 'What happens at Uvos, stays in Uvos.'"

She went and did it, took photographs and everything for her newsletter in America. That was where her bread and butter came from. You gotta keep 'em fed and edgy up north.

I remember one time she posed in front of our big cargo boat, overloaded with food and supplies for a group. She had her assistant take pictures of her by the boat and then inside the boat, showing all the food and supplies. The photos ended up in her newsletter. She was giving donations to the poor villagers with a very worried look on her face.

I forget where Carmen and I were when her sister Gloria called all agitated and hysterical. "Turn on the radio. The head of the fishing association is yelling about el gringo Norman Walters. He says that you cut the nets in Uvos Cocha with the Dolphin Lady and the Forest Police. He says they will kill you, and that you destroyed thousands of soles worth of nets."

Well, damned if you do and damned if you don't, eh? We did turn on the radio, and he was still ranting and raving worse than Rush Limbaugh, and yes, he did make a threat. He said that they would be waiting for me in the mouth of the Rio Yarapa, and they would have their revenge. WTF? I didn't do a GD thing, and he said that I was her partner. That was the worst insult that he could have hit me with.

I decided to get educated on what the "fishing association" really was. Come to find out this little club is synonymous with…da, da…the (fucking) Fishing Mafia. It's always good to know who you are dealing with, right, Don Corleone?

I had shotguns and a revolver that shot true. What I didn't have was an AR-15 or an AK-47. Were they going to have them? I didn't have any guests that week, so we took off from Iquitos on a song and a prayer. We had to enter from the mouth of the river, because walking from the Ucayali River to the Yarapa River in those days took twenty-five minutes with all the food and baggage for the week. Plus, *Yacuruna* would have to dock on the Ucayali, the driver would have to sleep in the boat, and he could be attacked in the night by the mafia or river pirates. It was not a good scenario. I decided to just bust through them at sixty miles per hour. It was my only option, come what may.

## CHASING THE DREAM

As we neared the mouth of the Rio Yarapa, there appeared to be quite a few boats tied up at the banks on both sides. We were quite a ways off, and I was using binoculars, so I devised a plan. I motioned to the driver to slow to twenty knots. Maybe I could fool them. All the villagers knew that we were usually "balls to the wall" or "flat out" coming to the lodge. We'd have been traveling for almost three hours, and I would want to be home. So…if this boat wasn't Sr. Norman's boat, they might let their guard down. We did leave earlier than normal so as not to be arriving at the regular hour, which was right before noon. It was only 10:30 and they weren't being vigilant yet.

We were only about seventy yards from the boats when they started taking notice of *Yacuruna*. It would take them time to react, start their motors, get their boats headed in the right direction, and head out at ten to fifteen knots, their top speed, so I yelled "GOOOO!"

Eleodoro put the pedal to the metal and the *proa* (bow) raised like an airplane. We were going sixty miles per hour in a matter of seconds, and when we passed the flotilla of boats they were still fifty feet away from us on either side. They were all waving machetes, yelling; I saw only a few single-shot shotguns, no automatics. I motioned for everyone to get down and only heard two shots go off. We were so far away by then that the shot just bounced off of the aluminum boat like BBs. WE DID IT!

In the next month or so, I had my guys spread the word to all the villages that I wasn't even on the Yarapa when the travesty happened, and I would never have cut up their livelihood. Everyone knew that I had different ways of doing things. I always tried to reason with the local people, bringing my thoughts and beliefs of ecology and preservation.

Listen, my thoughts were: not to net up the mouth of the lake because that would capture the dolphins too. Duh, they would get hungrier and hungrier and eat about everything they saw, ripping the nets to shreds. If they could leave, they would go where there were easier pickings.

In about four trips there weren't any boats lying in wait for us at all. We went our merry way, amen. (And I only had to kill three men and wound four women in that month. Not bad, eh?)

Just kidding…

• • •

We all made it through the lean months up to Christmas. We had quite a few guests and enjoyed the two-week RHP group. Watching them grow into their groove was cool—Hospital Yacumama.

When Yamuna and John were at the lodge, she taught the cooks to make tofu and falafel. My dishes for the guests were almost all Peruvian dishes, tweaked a bit so as not to be too greasy, too sweet, or too salty. I taught them to make pancakes, omelets, French toast, scrambled eggs (like clouds), and oatmeal (the way North Americans eat them). Our food had as many compliments as our excursions in the guest book.

Carmen's family shared Christmas with us at the lodge, and then it was time for the New Year's Eve group (twenty guests). Oh boy, was that ever something. I brought up a local music group from the pueblo, drums and flute; it was jungle music, jungle beat. We danced—even Carmen's father, Don Teddy, cut a rug—did the limbo, the train, and the hop. We made popcorn and all the guests brought out their candy; we had beer and mixed drinks, and at midnight Carmen and I brought out the champagne. A good time was had by all, because the workers joined in too.

We entered a new year with all the good projections anyone could muster. The groups were going to grow again for this season, and I had to build five more bungalows. We were cruisin', and there would be another

## CHASING THE DREAM

*Don Teddy: New Year's Eve*

RHP group in February. It was a hell of a lot of work, but we were definitely chasing the dream to wherever it would take us.

*Carmen and Norman:
New Year's Eve*

**PART 10**
# THE TOWER TO THE SKY
*Yacumama Lodge*
*Spring 1996*

# FIFTEEN

**WE ZIPPED THROUGH THE BUILDING** of the five bungalows. The river was on our side that year and did not rise to record levels (a good off-season for FIT travel also). The RHP group went well, without a hitch. They were refining their system. The doctors, nurses, medical students, and volunteers were awesome.

One of my fondest memories of the Peruvian staff was when the food came out and it was something that they were not accustomed to, the Peruvian Dr. Alex would look at me and ask, "*¿Qué es este nuevo alimento que estamos a punto de comer?*" (What is this new food that we are about to eat?)

I'd laugh and say, "*Abrir tu mente, Alex, nuevas experiencias son buenas.*" (Open your mind, Alex, new experiences are good.)

He and his associates would laugh and load up their plates. Believe it or don't, they did become accustomed to the "*nueva lengua*" (new tongue), and they did "open their minds."

• • •

We were reaching late March when my friend from CET emailed me and asked if I had any intentions of augmenting the experiences for the students at Yacumama Lodge this upcoming season. Previously we had discussed "more diverse things to do" in our talks at the lodge.

Being the guy that I was (and still am), I thought about it a bit and responded, "Sure, I'll have a surprise for you all this season. How about a 115-foot-tall tower, a seventy-five-foot zip line to a remote platform, and another zip line back to the main tower?"

As you can imagine, we were the number one pleasers again. I failed to mention that I had already designed and discovered the location for the tower, and that Lawrence had scheduled Mike Weis and Paul Sibley (creators of Extreme Productions, the rigging company responsible for the zip line in the movie *Medicine Man* with Sean Connery) to arrive and help with the feasibility and rigging design for the zip line.

Mike would arrive in a few days to teach me the art, magic, and safety of ascending-descending-and-traversing with ropes and equipment, while Paul would follow two weeks later to help design and construct the actual zip line. In the two-week space I had to build the tower.

Mike Weis arrived as planned with his son and a couple of others. I took them to the tree that we had selected. The base, where the roots entered the ground, was over twenty-five feet in diameter with stabilizing roots as big around as a ten-year-old's body, which ran on top of the ground at least seventy-five to one hundred feet in all directions from the main trunk. It was about 140 feet tall and the soundest tree my guys could find. I had sent three groups of three men into the jungle to search for the most magnificent tree in our proximity. It took one week, and it turned out that it resided a twenty-minute walk from the lodge.

## CHASING THE DREAM

*Absolutely perfect*

He loved the tree and looked up, upper, and uppermost to the top of the tree. He stretched out his arm and pointed to a confluence of branches about 110 feet up, which formed a natural nest. He looked at me, smiled, and said, "That nest will cradle the top platform."

I already figured out weeks before that to make things work, we had to start at the top and then build up to it if we wanted to be ready for Paul to install the zip line when he arrived. My incredible guide, Octavio Santana (purebred Yagua blood), could do anything I asked. I took him to the tree, and he told me that it was a *zapote renaco*, a type of strangler fig. I pointed to the nesting place. He formed a circle with each of his hands by touching his thumb to his index and middle fingers, therefore creating his binoculars. He raised his two hands to his eyes and peered at the nest. I'd seen him do this many times, and he always dazzled the guests with his ability to see and point out animals that they had difficulty seeing with their Bausch and Lomb's.

"Octavio," I said, "please make me a bow that you would be able to shoot an arrow with a rope attached over and through the top of that nest."

"Okay," he answered, and we walked back to the lodge in silence.

**Note: These next few paragraphs may be a bit tedious to some, but try to suffer through them. They explain a lot.**

The next day at breakfast, after Mike arrived, I told him that I had the man to shoot an arrow over the top of the tree. I sent for Octavio, and he came to the main lodge with the bow and arrow. It was crafted from cumaceba wood and had a braided *chambira* (palm leaf fiber) bowstring. The arrow was a reed from the Rio Ucayali and feathers he had found in the jungle. Dude, that was impressive.

We trekked to our tree, hauling one hell of lot of climbing gear. I guess we were starting the training today—okay with me, because I had to get this jungle-experience-surprise finished in about nine weeks, when the first CET group would arrive.

I had ordered all the wood for the designed tower weeks in advance to be sure we had what we needed when we needed it. All dimensional lumber is cut thirteen feet long in Peru, so that was to be the height of each story going up.

But today we were not thinking about construction. We were

## CHASING THE DREAM

thinking about climbing 110 feet up on one-half-inch rope with mechanical ascenders called jumars, hand-held clamps that are attached to a fixed rope and automatically tighten when weight is applied and relax when pushed up. It is kind of hard to understand unless you are doing it. These simple devices allow you to ascend a rope from ground level to whatever height you desire using your own strength (twelve to sixteen inches for every push you make). You have to be kind of strong, though, because you have a looped sling for your foot to be connected to one jumar ascender on the rope. You use this as a push-point for each incremental ascent you make. The other jumar ascender is connected about eighteen inches above the first jumar, for advancing up the rope with every push you make.

Octavio had attached fishing weights to the tip of the arrow to give it enough weight to fall to the ground after being shot over the tree nest at 110 feet above the ground. Mike attached a very strong but thin cord to the feather end of the arrow, and we gave Octavio the go-ahead to fire away.

His first try was a bit short, so he tightened the bowstring and prepared for the second round. He pulled back, aimed, and let go. Up the arrow went, perfectly through the confluence of branches, and fell to the ground at our feet. Gol-dang-it man, he did it! We laughed, danced around a bit, and tied the real rope to the cord. Mike pulled it back up the tree, over the nest, and back down again, tying it off on a very substantial root.

Now it was time for him to climb 110 feet to the nest, tie off the rope, and drop it down for me to climb. We would have two ropes to ascend for building. In our spare time, he had instructed me in the art of ascending and descending the tree and how to use the tool devices safely.

*Mike Weis, halfway up*

Mike hooked his two jumar ascenders to the rope and started climbing. Yes, it was a slow process, pulling your body 110 feet straight up against gravity. It took him about six to eight minutes to reach the nest. He unhooked his ascenders and tied off the rope that he had climbed up. He moved to another branch higher than the nest and affixed a large pulley, threaded a rope through it, and let the two ends fall to the ground. This rope would be for the materials we had to pull up.

Now it was my turn to ascend the tree. I hooked up and started up. Push-pull, push-pull, push-pull…and after about five minutes of this action I had to take a small breather.

It took me ten minutes to reach the top where Mike was sitting. Now, in my jungles I have found more than one way to skin a jaguar (figuratively speaking, of course). I actually used this second method quite a few times when the limbs were too high to shoot an arrow over.

Just like climbing any old tree, but be sure to tie off! You know, that reminds me of the time (I am meandering now, jumping ahead a few years) Alexander Krstevski (an environmental advocate), Jim Cronk (the CET guy),

*Just hanging out*

# CHASING THE DREAM

*Richard, Nixon, and Norman*

and Peter Gros (the Wild Kingdom guy), came to do a research project funded partially by CET, the Explorers' Club, and Mutual of Omaha on the "Relationship of Epiphytic Concentration in Tropical Rainforest Architecture." In layman's terms, where and how bromeliads live, wild, in the rainforests. It was a good experience.

Anyway, Alex (arriving in a week) needed a tree that was close to the riverbank, had a large population of bromeliads, and was an emerging canopy tree at least 150 feet tall. I found the tree right across the river from Yacumama Lodge. It was at least 175 feet tall, the first branches at 135 feet, a large quantity of vines, and maybe three different areas of bromeliads.

I suited up and went to the tree with my crew (Richard and Nixon, their real names).

I set up with the bow and arrow that Octavio had made for me, made three attempts, and was shy of reaching the first branches by twenty feet. There were other alternatives: levitate, fly, or climb. I picked the only rational one: fly. No, really, I climbed up the vines.

I did take a bunch of stuff with me, so I was kind of weighted down. There was a 200-foot rope, a descender, a backpack of climbing accessories, camera, repellent, and water. The vines were the size of my bicep, alive and strong, and there were good footholds, so I was confident for my climb. There is nothing secure about rotting or dead vines.

It actually takes a lot more energy to climb up a tree without using ascenders, so I tied off every so often, had a sip of water, rested my muscles, and then continued on, pulling myself up the tree hand over hand. About halfway up I stopped to rest, tied off, and was taking a sip of water when I was hit in the ankle with the full swing of a Louisville Slugger, or so it seemed. I was tied off in two different places, so when I lost my handhold grabbing for my foot, and then lost my footing too, I was at the mercy of the nylon webbing and the vines. They were my friends and they held tight while I was swinging seventy-five feet above the ground.

I looked down at my leg, and to my surprise there were a few of those inch-long *izula* or bullet ants crawling around, looking for another place to strike. Oh yeah, I remembered them, all right. In the early days on the Yarapa, Lawrence and I had a taste of their venom. I quickly brushed them off with my gloved hand. I've been bitten and stung by a lot of badass neighbors, but these were the worst. The quicker you get to the afflicted area, the better, but I was hanging by a couple of nylon threads, with excruciating pain and panic.

I pulled it together, looked to where I had been standing, and saw thirty or forty ants. Okay, slow it all down. I raised my hands up to the nylon webbing, grabbed hold and pulled myself up, above the ant nest. I mean really, a giant animal crushes your house, and you are going to sit and take it? I'm sorry, guys.

I got my body above the havoc, found a foothold nowhere near the ants, tied off in *three* places, and bent to view the damage. I had my safari pants tucked into my socks, so I pulled the sock down, jerked the pant leg up, and saw a familiar picture: five white bumps, like

## CHASING THE DREAM

edamame under the skin. I didn't have a cigarette on me, but I for sure had some Captain Black nicotine in my system, and that just might work. I pulled the lizard out, twisted my ankle around, and let go with the urine flow. See, that is why you should drink at least eight ounces of water an hour when in the jungle. I saturated my shoe and sock too, but I didn't give a shit. It would counteract the poison and calm the pain. I just prayed that I hadn't waited too long to attend to the stings. That is the beauty of osmosis and other naturally occurring marvels of this Earthsuit. Some things do work, and it was working.

Just a little side note here: Naylita was stung by a man-o-war jellyfish one time when we were visiting my family in Florida. Beautiful beach, warm sand, good company, and the kids were playing in the surf. I noticed Nayla coming out of the water, rubbing her hands up and down her legs like she was washing them. Then I saw her face, jumped up and ran for the water.

I knew exactly what had happened, and I looked around for someone smoking. A girl, twenty feet away. I ran to her and asked for a cigarette. She gave me one and I ran back to Nayla. Carmen was on her way to her daughter by that time, for she was screaming and crying. I noticed her bright-red inflamed legs and crushed the cigarette in my hand, telling her to pee. She was about seven or eight, but didn't blink an eye, just let it go through her bathing suit. I caught it, mixed it with the tobacco, and rubbed it all over her thighs and calves. We held her between us, and in about three minutes she stopped thrashing and crying. Fifteen minutes later, she was back in the surf playing with her cousin Joey. A large percentage of people stung by these man-o-war jellyfish have to go to the hospital for treatment.

Okay, back to it.

I communicated to my crew what had happened, and they wanted me to come down. No way! Within five minutes I could maintain and began climbing again. I reached the area with the bromeliads, tied off, and was presented with a very prominent limb as a walkway through the cascading epiphytes. This was a perfect place for Alex's research. I attached a lifeline on the limbs above to snap onto, tied off the rope for ascending and descending, and took a look at the view.

*YACUMAMA LODGE from 175 feet*

• • •

When Alex and his group arrived, I introduced them to the "tower" and demonstrated the safe use of the climbing equipment that he would be using. Then it was time for the real test. We would start the next day after breakfast. Alex would ascend the tree, and the rest of the group would go on excursions in the wild jungle.

One fond memory: when Alex was on his way to the top branches, feeling great and in his element, he held the Explorer's Club flag up for a picture. Jim captured it perfectly.

Alex completed his research (I still have his paper and his business card), and I was glad to be involved.

# CHASING THE DREAM

*Peter Gros and Jim Cronk*

*Alex Krstevski and Norman*

# SIXTEEN

**BACK TO THE TOWER.** I was ascending that tree with Mike to evaluate the location for the top platform, nestled in the branches. When I reached him I noticed that there was so much light at this altitude. Everything opened up, and I could see above the canopy. I flashed back to my words and thoughts years before: "I will see above the canopy one day, and on to Brazil." There were paradise tanagers and other special birds flying around us. I was perched in a separate reality, something new and exciting.

*Mike Weis and Norman Walters at 110 feet "UP"*

Mike was used to this kind of life, so he was relaxing in one of the crotches, but for me, my dreams were coming true so I wasn't relaxed, I was jazzed!

The next step was setting the pulley system up to facilitate the raising of posts, beams, and joists (all called *vigas* in Spanish).

## CHASING THE DREAM

Mike designed the system and taught us how to rope the planks and haul them up to their desired positions. This platform was the hardest because it was the highest. Steve Shephard (man of the white rivers) and Jim Cronk (CET) assumed the "ground man" position at different times and controlled the men who were pulling the ropes, raising the wooden beams.

Steve assured all the ropes were secure before they started their "heave-ho" process, lifting the 500-pound vigas 110 feet into the air. We did it! We built the crotch-supported platform, the highest point, 115 feet above the ground.

Now we were returning to the ground to start the building of the tower. We had quite a few weeks left before the first CET group arrived, but we had a ton of heavy work to do. I had a crew of twelve guys—sixteen including Mike, Steve, Jim, and me.

*Richard and me at 115 feet, finishing the top platform*

We bought all of Mike's equipment: ropes, ascenders, descenders, pulleys, carabiners up the yin-yang, brakes, and more climbing ropes. He left a happy man. Paul Sibley was arriving in about a week and a half to design and install the zip line. We had to shake a tail feather, baby!

Our first order of business was to build the seven platforms to the sky, decide the best location to construct the receiving platform of the zip line, install the line, and test it. It would be a lot of ascending with jumars, hanging from ropes attached to our harnesses (a real ball-busting dance), installing Lincoln-Log-type uprights and beams floor by floor, 100 feet into the canopy, and drilling—bolting it all together (illustrated below).

This is where the real coordination was needed. You can see in the last picture the 300-pound horizontal beam that is hanging in front of me, ready to fit into the notched posts. Richard is hanging at the other post, ready to receive the beam. If you look closely, you will see little Nayla on the platform, helping.

**A N D...**

**CHASING THE DREAM**

## VOILA!

*Over ten stories tall, solid hardwood*

This is how it all started. Of course, later we installed roofs. I built this in six weeks with twelve men and a little girl, LOL.

Four days later, Paul Sibley arrived. We got right on it and began the zip line. Since he had worked on the movie *Medicine Man* and was accustomed to working in the wilds, I gave him my seal of confidence and trusted him wholly. We had to project and imagine where the zip line would go and where it would return.

Paul stood on the highest platform in the tree and looked around 360 degrees. There was another tall tree about seventy-five feet from his vantage point, with a branch to support a hanging receiving platform in the correct location. From there we could send the exhilarated guests back to the main tower, two stories below the starting point. It looked good to me.

I had to figure out the logistics: arrive at the location in the second tree, set up the pulley system to haul the building materials for the platform up, and string the rope across the void. Paul and I worked out all the steps involved, and Richard and I ascended, built, and set up the bones of the operation.

Paul selected the equipment—that we had purchased from Mike—that would work for the joy ride, and set the whole system up to work for any guest desiring to "feel the rush."

When he left, the arrival at the remote platform (seventy-five feet away from the tower) was still a bit iffy, but it worked. I had to receive the riders (almost lying down) and send them back to the tower from the remote platform with a change of ropes and a Hail Mary.

After I became literate to the workings of the equipment and the system, I changed it so the riders could arrive at the remote platform standing on their own two feet. That was a winner and less work for me.

This was a real improvement for the recurring groups of the Children's Environmental Trust, year to year. The preparation for the zip line was rigorous: strapping on the harnesses, understanding how it all worked, and ascending, by

# CHASING THE DREAM

stairs, a ten-story building. What a hardy bunch of guests we had. There were only a few not able to complete the climb or the ride: "Unhappy Faces."

As you can imagine, "The Tower to the Sky" was a hit!

We all enjoyed the tower and zip line, every year getting better and better with little adjustments. In the next several years I was visited by my older daughter Star, my older son Luke, my cousin Rochelle's son Bill, Lawrence's son Cassidy, and various other "helpers" sent to assist me with the groups. Some turned out good, some flopped. I dealt with it.

It was great having family around, reminiscing, explaining, helping them remember their earlier lives, and eating together. Some of the boys fit right into the Iquitos scene; others stayed away from it, spending most of their weekends at the lodge. This was good, having a sense of managerial authority in the lodge in my absence, and having the lodge made up and ready for the entering weekly groups.

Star was with me for the shortest amount of time and returned to Iquitos on the weekends

*My daughter Star having fun!*

with me. It was hard for her because she was into jogging. Well, take a look at her picture: every time she jogged around our neighborhood there'd be a pack of wolves after her, if you know what I mean.

*My son Luke leaving the remote platform*

• • •

Our groups were getting larger and larger, and it seemed as though the dice were rolling in our favor. We had the *Yacuruna* speedboat remodeled into a small *rapido* (a boat used to move people on the river) which held about eight passengers, and commissioned the naval base to build us a thirty-five-foot boat that would hold over twenty-four passengers, the new *Yacumama III*.

*Nayla and Norman...zippin'*

We had constructed the *Yacumama II*, a thirty-five-foot wooden boat, ourselves years before at the lodge for our weekly cargo boat. I'll tell you, those four Macuyama brothers were great wooden boat builders and good friends also.

Poncho had a cantina in Puerto Miguel where we partied; Lucho and Miguel were reliable carpenters; and I remember Manuel

**CHASING THE DREAM**

Macuyama as the man with a perpetual smile on his face, but all of them were exceptional boat builders for the community.

*Yacumama III*

# NORMAN WALTERS

*Manuel Macuyama with a load of leaf*

**PART 11**
# A CLOSE CALL
*Iquitos To Miami*
*1996-1997*

# SEVENTEEN

**IN MARCH OF 1996,** Carmen started getting headaches. They weren't debilitating at first, and we just wrote it off as bad headaches. By May, when I was starting the construction of the tower, they turned into really bad headaches that lasted a week or two. I was starting to think they were migraines that could possibly have been caused by her having to plan for our wedding. Yes, that's right, we were going to make it real, get married, and live "happily ever after." Kooo, baby!

Our wedding was planned for June 8, 1996. We'd been together for over three years, and things were looking good for us. We were functioning as a family. The headaches were gone, but for the two weeks that pain had visited her (very bad guests) she wasn't able to eat. So by the time our wedding came around, she was as beautiful as ever, just a bit thin.

My friend Willy drove us around the city before our wedding in his new taxi—tin cans tied to the back bumper and streamers flying in the rain. Yes, you guessed it right again, it stormed the night of our wedding. That could have been a warning, but it didn't dampen our spirits. A great band, a lot of booze, all our friends and acquaintances were there, and we danced our arses off. My favorite song at that time was "Oye Mi Amor" by Mana, and when the band played it as our wedding song, Carmen and I tore up the floor. At one point, I grabbed her and swung her off her feet.

*My Princess of Iquitos*

## CHASING THE DREAM

We passed the summer with groups and a few family outings. In the fall, Carmen had a worse encounter with the unwanted guest: pain. There was a RHP medical group coming in the first part of October, and I was praying that she could hold on until then. At this point she could not keep anything down, nausea pills did not work, she couldn't be in a lighted room, and no one could figure out her problem. One Iquitos doctor told her that she was pregnant. Yes, pregnant women could have these symptoms. The only problem with his diagnosis: She had her period at the time of his evaluation. Another doctor told her that she had giardia from parasitic water. I still had to work with the tourists, leaving every Sunday morning and returning Friday afternoon. She basically just lay in bed—in pain. The family helped a bit with Naylita, and Carmen did her best, getting her ready for school, fed, and washed.

Then one week I received an emergency radio call at the lodge. We had been robbed the night before. In these times, almost every house had a little open space in the roof in the middle of their house called a *juerta* or little garden. This opening would let the cooking smoke out; now they all have metal bars. The robbers would throw rags inside the house saturated with chloroform, then cover up the opening in the roof with blankets and wait for everyone to be unconscious.

They stole everything of value from houses, even the sheets and pillows from the beds. I am talking TVs, stereo, food, furniture, and worst of all, purses. Carmen woke up and noticed that everything looked different—blank walls and a strange smell in the house. She got up and checked on Nayla. She was on the bare mattress, still asleep, not able to rouse, and most of her clothes and toys were gone from her drawers and shelves.

Our two TVs were gone, the stereo system, small appliances, food, and $500 from Carmen's purse. So Carmen had to deal with the pain in her head as well as the robbery. She has five brothers, so they secured the place and repaired the things that were broken. We knew exactly who did it: our housekeeper's boyfriend's gang. No kidding, and the real kicker: Nothing was ever found, and no one was ever apprehended. Ahhh, whatever. We moved to a more secure (?) neighborhood shortly after.

At our next rental, I built a wrought iron birdcage around the vulnerable areas. The robbers did try, but were not able to break through my security…curses, foiled again.

The medical group came, and I took Carmen to the lodge. She was still suffering, but there were U.S. doctors there, and they had all kinds of medicines. Just maybe…

After much evaluation by those learned doctors, it was determined that it could be migraine headaches. There is actually a self-administered injection (sort of like an EpiPen for allergies) that they had with them. The only problem was, they only had a couple due to the fact that they were personal, for one of the doctors suffering from migraines.

Okay, let's try one. Bam…and it helped a bit. I believed that they were just powerful pain relievers, nothing magical. I was right; the shot deadened the pain for a while, but it recurred. It ended up that they couldn't help her. They went home; the pain retreated again, and Carmen was normal. This time she was clear for three months before it raised its ugly head and rendered her a moaning invalid. This was very heartbreaking to watch, for she could have been dying, and there was no technology in Peru to help her. No CT scans, no MRI.

She had another episode in the summer of 1997, and I had to hospitalize her for a short period. She was getting thinner, weighing about eighty-nine pounds. Her short bouts of eating were not enough to counteract the weight loss from the attacks. Her aunt Rosa was a registered nurse at the naval hospital, and we asked her to send a naval doctor to see Carmen at the Clinica Ana Stahl.

## CHASING THE DREAM

He arrived, asked her questions, looked in her eyes, checked her pulse, and said, "Are you traveling to the U.S.A. in the near future?"

I responded. "We are planning a trip in the fall."

"Well, I would suggest that you immediately contact a neurologist upon arrival. Get MRI and CT imaging done. There may be an irregularity in your brain," he said, looking at Carmen.

We thanked him, and he left. We looked at each other, and Carmen's eyes watered up, probably from the pain as much as from the news. I held her, and luckily she couldn't see my face or my tearing eyes. When I was more or less back to normal, I told her I would take care of it and not to worry. What else could I say?

My son Luke and I finished out the summer groups, and Carmen's pain left again. I settled everything at the lodge and finished the last arrangements for our trip to Miami, Florida. Luke, Naylita, Carmen, and I were flying to Miami, and my daughter Star was flying in the day after we arrived. We were going to have a big vacation. We deserved it.

The day we were to fly to Miami, Carmen started having pain in her head again. It was a good thing that we had packed the day before. It was a mid-morning flight to Miami. Carmen didn't look good, but we made it onto the plane, got seated, and she leaned her head onto my shoulder. Luke was okay. Naylita was great, on her first long airplane ride. Of course we had been going to Lima for years, but that was just an hour and a half flight. This was four and a half hours, with a meal and a movie. Big time!

Lawrence and Adriana were living in Coral Gables at that time, and we were going to be staying at their house. They had extra bedrooms, and we would only be there for a couple of days. They picked us up at the airport, and they could tell immediately that Carmen was under attack. She wasn't in full-on attack mode yet, but really hurting.

Star was to arrive in a few hours. Lawrence, Luke, and I would go to pick her up, and Adriana would stay with Carmen and Nayla at the house. After that I would have to figure what we were going to do. Everything was going topsy-turvy on me. Not what we had planned. These attacks usually lasted two to three weeks, so that would be the end of our vacation.

But you know something? Human nature is a strange thing. If Carmen hadn't had an actual attack on this trip, would I have been as zeroed in on her condition? Probably not!

Soooo...we picked up Star, drove back to the house, and checked in with Adriana. Carmen was not good. Throwing up even though there was nothing in her system—dry, baby, dry. Water, ice, juice, and most of it came up. You can forget food; it was only provoking the dragon. We didn't know who the dragon was. I was shooting in the dark. Medical training...not! Technology...yes!

I went up to the bedroom. All the blinds were drawn, it was dark, and she was crying. It was already too late to get any response from a pedigreed neurologist; after all, it was 3:30 in the afternoon—nothing but message machines. I gave her a hug and said, "I will take care of this in the morning."

I went back downstairs, got the kids together, and told them the bad news. Our vacation would be the best I could make it for them. They were to stay for one week, and we would do whatever we could. But the first order of business was getting Carmen relieved of this monster. Everyone agreed that was the first line of defense.

● ● ●

Monday morning, 10:00 a.m. came around. I had my coffee, Lawrence and I had talked about our scheduling, and I was ready to get a doctor

## CHASING THE DREAM

to see Carmen. The first hour and a half was very depressing. I explained the situation and the urgency I felt, and the best I could obtain was an appointment four weeks in the future. At this time there were agencies in the phone book for every single thing that you were searching. I decided—screw them. I would call every neurologist in the Miami phone book.

Believe it or don't, but I decided to use my intuition to pick the doctor to help my Carmen. There had to be a hundred "brain doctors," and I just went down the list with my finger on each name, trying to feel the energy of each person. I know this seems like a real "mumbo-jumbo" thing to do, but I have lived my life trying to listen to my inner voice, and have been rewarded many times for doing so.

A...B...C...nothing. D...E...F...shit, man, nada, nothing. G...H...I...nothing. That was a lot of damn names. I relaxed a bit, took a few deep breaths, and started again. J...nothing, K...nothing, and in the first part of L, I felt it. Dr. Alberto Lacayo. Okay, I would make the call now! You gonna do it, do it all the way!

I dialed the number and a woman answered, asking me how she could help me. I explained, in English, our situation, and the urgency I felt for the appointment. She took a few more data points from me, and asked me to hold.

"Hello, this is Alberto Lacayo. I have your information here. Could you explain a bit more about what has transpired in the last year and a half, and how it started?"

I explained, as I have explained to all of you in detail (leaving out the robbery, of course, LOL).

He thought for a moment and asked, "When can you bring your wife in?"

I was flabbergasted. "Er...uh... Now?"

"Where are you located?"

"Coral Gables," I responded.

Silence... "We're close, how about forty-five minutes?"

"Really?" I asked. "I have been trying to get an appointment for an hour and a half, and nobody has the time for me."

"Señor, you are talking to the right person now."

I thanked him and ran up the stairs to give the news to Carmen. She was dry heaving when I walked in, so I waited a bit, relayed the story, and asked her to get ready. YEE HAW, BABY!

As we entered Dr. Lacayo's office, I noticed serene paintings of water, beaches, and forests on the walls. It was very simple, though, and I wondered if we were on the right path. I looked around, noticing that there were no other people in the waiting room. I signed in, and we sat down.

"Carmen Walters?" came the request.

We followed her down a hall and into an examination room. She smiled at Carmen, turned, and left the room, closing the door. Not even five minutes later, Dr. Lacayo opened the door and entered. He introduced himself, shook our hands, took the folder from the door file slot, closed the door, and sat down. He opened the file and began writing.

"In your own words, tell me how all of this began, and how it progressed up to now."

Carmen explained the whole experience the best she could to the doctor in Spanish. He was taking notes, looking up at her every minute or so. When she was done, he leaned back in his chair, closed his eyes, and appeared to be concentrating.

"Let's take a look," he said. "I want to check a few things. Sit here and look forward. I want to look into your eyes." He shone his lighted instrument in one eye and then the other, looked in both ears, felt and counted her pulse, sat back down, and told her to relax.

I reluctantly began, "Carmen was examined by a very good

## CHASING THE DREAM

Peruvian doctor from the naval hospital. His only advice was to get to the U.S. and have her brain imaged with an MRI or a CT scan."

"Yes, we need to do that first. There is a possibility that you may have a brain tumor. The only way to tell is to take an image and see what is in there. The extreme pain is what is odd. Would you be able to go to the Baptist Hospital now for CT and MRI imaging?"

The good doctor called in a prescription because he was affiliated, and I asked, "How much do I owe for today?"

He just smiled at me and said, "Let's just see what we have first."

We made our way to the Baptist Hospital, checked in, filled out all the papers, waited about fifteen minutes, and they called Carmen's name for the MRI scan. I gave her a hug and a kiss, and she disappeared through the door. This took some time to set up and get going. I was placed in the waiting area, but I could see the chamber. She looked small inside that big machine. This was 1997, and I had been in Peru for five years. I didn't know this technology even existed. X-rays, sure, but magnetic resonance? That was stretching it a bit. I had to get up to speed quickly.

You have to lie totally still, no jewelry, no gum, no shoes, no shirt, no problem! Ho ho… There was a control room with four or five guys behind glass, looking at the imaging. I guess for early detection or something. She was about fifteen minutes into it when the energy changed in the room. I could feel it. Then I saw two more technicians gather around one of the screens, looking and pointing at the screen. I wasn't going to take this any longer. I walked to the door and tried the knob; it wasn't locked. I opened the door and barged in.

"Hey, you're not supposed to be in here," one pencil-neck said.

"That is my wife, and I *am* in here," I shot back.

He tried to cover the screen, but I had seen it, and my eyes were my camera in those days. I still have the image engraved in my mind as I am writing this. I walked to the screen, and the tech backed away. There on the screen was my wife's brain, with a white mass the size of my fist occupying most of her left brain, pushing everything into the right side. It looked very uncomfortable and dangerous. No wonder she was in pain!

"What is this?" I said, pointing at the white mass. "What could this be?"

He guardedly said, "I don't know, but you shouldn't be in here. It is off limits."

"We have to call Dr. Lacayo. He has to see this," I said.

"I am only a radiologist; you have to talk to them outside or call your doctor," he said.

I looked very carefully again, turned around and left the room. I walked straight to the main desk and asked to use the phone. I called Dr. Alberto Lacayo and told him the situation. He told me that he would be there in five minutes, he was on site, and to sit down and breathe.

Dr. Lacayo burst through the swinging doors, came over to me and put a hand on my shoulder. "I will look and try to see what we have. Just sit tight, and I will call you in."

I sat down, watching the people behind the glass. I could see the doc looking at the screen and the radiologist explaining something to him. He came out of the glass room and asked me, "Did you see the image?"

I answered, "Yes, and what can we do?"

"I am calling a specialist in tropical medicine to look at the images. Dr. Jose Perez has been dealing with tropical diseases of Central and South America for years, and he is a friend of mine. For now, let's move her into the CT scan room, so we can better understand what we are dealing with. Dr. Perez is in the hospital, and will be able to study the imaging while she is in the CT chamber."

## CHASING THE DREAM

In she went, there I sat, and out she walked about twenty-five minutes later. Done! I called Dr. Lacayo, and he told me to bring Carmen to a designated waiting lounge. They explained that the mass was very big, and had taken over almost half of her brain. Her sight was being affected, and the nerve and muscle movement on the right side of her body was being slightly compromised.

Dr. Lacayo began by stating, "What is in there is undisclosed by the imaging. The mass could be a tumor, but to make sure I would have to perform a biopsy. This means we would have to drill through your skull, insert an instrument, and remove a piece of the mass. I know you are here from Peru on vacation and have no U.S. insurance. This would be expensive, and Dr. Perez has informed me that he believes that it could be the nest of a parasite."

Dr. Perez took over. "The technical name for this infestation is neurocysticercosis, and is from the ingestion of eggs of *taenia solium* (pork tapeworm) due to contamination of food by people with *taeniasis*, and by ingesting undercooked pork. Neurocysticercosis is the most common parasitic disease of the nervous system in developing countries, and can develop into acquired epilepsy."

Now the kicker of the situation was: To perform a biopsy, Dr. Lacayo would have to perforate the tumor to obtain a sample. If the mass was an encapsulated nest of the parasite, and it was perforated, it could—or would—pollute her brain cavity and kill her, quickly.

Dr. Perez had an idea: There was a drug that killed the parasite, *praziquantel* (this was 1997). He asked if we would be willing to admit her for eight days in a private room in the Baptist Hospital. Now, the BH was the most expensive hospital in Miami. The MRI had just cost us $1,300 and the CT scan $800. The room was to be $1,095 a day, and the pills were $65 each, plus she would have to have three more MRI and CT scans taken. But BH had the best reputation.

I said yes! (How to pay? Fuck it.)

He extrapolated her cure by the drug to be thirty-plus days. In eight days we would be able to see a change in the size of the nest, if in fact it was neurocysticercosis. Yes, it was an expensive gamble, but the other side of the coin was "losing the girl." If no change occurred, then we would know it was a tumor and proceed with that knowledge.

She stayed the eight days, and I spent most of them balancing my time between making sure Carmen was okay—she was scared as hell and weak as a kitten—trying to vacation with the older kids, and making sure Naylita was okay in the Coral Gables house. That is where Adriana shined, a gem of gems. Naylita watched kids' shows on TV, ate ice cream, ate her meals, and took naps. Adriana was her main caregiver. I was able to take everyone to visit my mom in Jupiter, Florida, go to the Sawgrass mall, and go out to eat a bit.

Luke and Star returned to Eugene, Oregon, feeling a bit neglected I'm sure, but we did have a time. Nayla gained a couple of pounds, Carmen was at eighty-nine pounds, and it was time for her next image scanning. We were going to see if the drug worked. So it was get out of the hospital bed, get dressed, and elevator down to the imaging rooms. I was waiting with bated breath. The drama had been pretty heavy for the last eight days—anticipation, anxiety, hope, and doubt. It was completed, and she would go back to the hospital room.

# EIGHTEEN

**I WENT BACK** to the observation room in the afternoon to see the imaging results. Carmen was feeling a little bit better. No more pain, she could eat a bit (without blowin' chunks), she'd seen Naylita (after eight days), and her eyes were a bit brighter. Sweet!

Dr. Lacayo, Dr. Perez, and I were in the viewing room. The radiologist entered with an assistant (hopefully he wasn't packing), and sat in his comfortable ergonomic chair. He had the old image and the new image side by side. They both had the fist-sized white mass in her brain. I looked at them, back and forth several times, and then looked at the two docs. They were looking also.

We were all let down when the radiologist said, "After looking at these two images, I've discerned that there has been no change." He looked at us dead-eyed.

"Would you place the new image exactly over the old image, please?" I asked.

"Certainly sir." He placed them both on the same pins, overlaying the two images *almost* perfectly.

Wait a minute. It looked weird; just a minute amount, but not perfect. Not as bad as a 3-D comic without the glasses, but there was something off. "Could you wait for five minutes, please?" I asked. "I have to get something out of my car." I had left my satchel in the car, and I had something in it that would either destroy or confirm my doubt.

I had a strong magnifying glass and a millimeter/inch measuring device. I entered the room and pulled out my tools. Everyone looked at me like I was crazy—everyone except the two docs. I walked up to the lighted screen, brought my glass into focus, and held my measuring device up to the screen. I was right: it was not an exact overlay. It was a very minute difference, but noticeable under the glass. Maybe 1/128th of an inch, or about ¼ millimeter, I don't know, but there was a difference.

If there was a difference, then there was a chance. I gave the radiologist a growl, saying, "I want a copy of all these images. I will pick them up tomorrow."

I conferred with the doctors and worked out a regimen: We would go on a twenty-four-day plan with the pills, two a day. We could go anywhere, but she was better not to travel too far or exert herself very much. She would get new MRI and CT scan imaging in fourteen days, have doctor's appointments, and we would see how the process was shaking out. This sounded like a plan.

Disney World, here we come. This was their first trip to the U.S. and we were going to enjoy our extended vacation. First, we would stay a few days with my mom, and they would finally meet.

Disney was great. Carmen was tired but feeling better and better, eating well, and gaining some weight. My mom, "Tutu" we called her, and Carmen and Nayla were a perfect fit—corn, beans, and red peppers: *succotash*.

My niece Jenny had a son, Joey, about the same age as Nayla. They became immediate friends even though they didn't speak the

## CHASING THE DREAM

same language. I remember one night Carmen and I went out with Jenny, and Nayla stayed home with Tutu. When we came home we saw them playing board games and the remains of a Hawaiian pizza on the counter. Boy oh boy, Tutu knew how to get to those kids. They communicated in the universal language of love.

The pills were a bitch, but Carmen did force them down, embedded in a piece of Mars Bar. It was the only way in the hospital that I had found for her to keep from ralphing them back up. She was looking really well when we went to Miami for the fourteen-day scans. Dr. Lacayo was there, Dr. Perez was there, and I was on the top of the world when I saw the image: the white mass was the size of my thumbnail. We all looked at each other and whooped it up.

By the time we were ready to return to Peru, the last scans displayed only a very small bit of scar tissue—maybe the size of Carmen's little toenail. They did it. Thank the Almighty Forces and the incredible human intelligence of two doctors: Lacayo and Perez. We will be eternally indebted to these two specialists.

Now I had to pay the piper, OMG...

I paid Dr. Alberto Lacayo and Dr. Jose Perez in cash. Their charges were actually much less than I had thought. The hospital was another story. Luckily I had very good credit and a Citi credit card that had an obscene credit limit. They gave me a traveling foreigner discount (Dr. Lacayo helped me with that), and I charged the whole thing: $25,000. They got their money, and I could pay it off at my leisure.

I was still married and had a wife. I knew it could have gone another way.

Okay, back to Peru, and the grind: YACUMAMA LODGE.

# PART 12
# POWERS THAT BE

*Yacumama Lodge*
*Late May 1998*

# NINETEEN

**IN VERY LATE MAY 1998** (coming closer now to Y2K), I was preparing for CET's first group of the year. It was to be forty-four young folk, eleven- to fourteen-year-olds, four college professors, and eight teachers/parents/staff, for a total of fifty-six guests. I believe some of them were probably from Noblesville, Indiana, one of my favorite groups, me being a Hoosier and all.

Like always, I was sitting in the spacious main building, what we called the *comedor* or dining/meeting room, at 5:00 a.m. (still dark), amidst a flurry of papers and schedules, when my main waiter-man, Wilson, came to me and exclaimed (I am going to translate here, to make things easier), "Señor Norman, your neighbor, Alicia, is here with her children. She is crying and wants to talk to you."

I looked down at the dock and turned to him. "Let her pass."

I watched as she approached, and I noticed that she and her four children looked shell-shocked. Disheveled and afraid.

I asked her and her children to take seats, and asked Wilson to bring coffee and refresco (fruit juice) for her children. I smiled at her, patted her shoulder, and asked her what was troubling her.

Her husband had died quite a few years earlier, and she had never taken up with another man. Therefore, the children were all her responsibility. Her house and land were just a stone's throw from the lodge on the opposite bank of the Yarapa River, so we were definitely neighbors. Whenever we had extra food, donated clothes, or money, I shared. To tell you the truth, older women in the world alone are one of my weak points.

"Señor Norman, last night many men, dirty and smelling of kerosene, entered my house. They had flashlights and guns, and they told me that they were going to use my house for a while."

Wilson brought the coffee and juice and poured for everyone.

"Did they harm you or were they abusive to you or your children?" I asked. Three of her children were girls.

"No, they weren't nice, but they did not hit us," she replied.

"So, what happened? How did you escape?"

"They came down the river ever so quietly in three aluminum boats packed with many full *costales* (rice bags). They dug a large hole behind my house, unloaded the costales, and hid them in the hole. This was in the *media noche* (middle of the night)."

"Okay, but how did you escape?"

"They had many strange-looking guns with long, curved things on the bottom. The bearded man told us to sit outside the house while the rest of them looked for food. When no one was watching us, we ran to the riverbank and got into the canoe. My daughter (pointing to her thirteen-year-old) pushed us off, and my son paddled away from our house. Here we all are."

Whew! That was a lot to swallow. In a few weeks, the first group of CET would be entering Yacumama Lodge, and I had a bunch of guys a minute and a half away from me with a ton (or more) of *pasta de coca* (cocaine base) in a hole and a few AK-47s. Well, that was pretty dramatic.

## CHASING THE DREAM

It was Friday, so we made a room up for Alicia and her kids. I assured her that she would be safe, and then left for Iquitos around noontime. I made sure the guys in the lodge had enough ammunition, and told them if they were overtaken, not to be heroes, just give up. Everything would work out okay, for I had a plan, and a timetable. Now all I needed was a drink...*clavo huasca*.

• • •

In the seven years that I had lived and roared in the upper Amazon, I had met some very important people and befriended them. DEA, CIA, and PNP (Peru National Police) were just a few. I met the alphabet agencies (from the USA) at Ari's Burger restaurant, had gotten to know them, traded stories, and became friendly with them over beer and food. They told me that if I ever had a problem with *narcotraficantes* (illicit drug people) to give them a call, transmit them the coordinates, and they would take it from there. I never thought I would need their help.

Around 1996, I thought it would be a good idea to get to know two of the most powerful people in Iquitos: the three-star general of the PNP and the head of immigration. I invited them to the lodge for the weekend, with their wives and any children, if they had them. They were all grown, thank you Lord.

They accepted, and we all had an enjoyable time. My father-in-law was my administrator at that time, and he knew everyone in Iquitos. My Spanish was getting better and better, so I could communicate, *bola-bola*. The immigration guy's wife had a chronic cough which had been bothering her since she moved to Iquitos (from Lima) months earlier.

Well, Don Teddy, my father-in-law and lodge boss, told her that he had just the thing for her: a remedy of cocona. He crushed the fruit that we had growing around the lodge, added lime juice and salt, and asked her to swallow small amounts by letting it run down her throat. They were there Friday through Sunday, and by the time she left she had no more cough. That was a winner; when we parted in Iquitos we were all happy travelers and good acquaintances.

In the years to come they both helped me with minor problems. The general invited Lawrence and me to his office for coffee and a toast (usually good scotch or whiskey) quite a few times, and to his house one time for lunch, all family included. He was known as the Drug Buster, and there was a price on his head. He brought many narcos in with tons and tons of pasta de coca. One day in his office, he took me aside and asked if I knew of any drug operations in the jungle upriver from us. I didn't, but he gave me his personal cell phone number and his direct office line and said, "If you ever come across any drug production, call me with the location and I will take care of it for you, my friend."

So I really had three aces in my hand. I drew the fourth when I decided to do something about it.

As I said, I had a plan. I talked to each of my aces and gave them a sketchy idea of what I had in mind. I told them I would contact them the following weekend to solidify the plan. Then I left Iquitos for the lodge on a fact-finding mission.

In the next few days, I had some of my most trusted workers from Puerto Miguel jaw around with the guys and bring back nuggets of information to me. I learned a lot in three days.

The narcos were enlisting the young boys of the villages to help them. A lot like the rebels in Colombia, and the mountains of Peru. They were also tempting the young girls with money and promises. There was quite a bit of canoe traffic up to Alicia's tambo.

I couldn't help but wonder how many pregnancies there would be in the villages after this reign of terror was over. I guessed that I should

## CHASING THE DREAM

move fast and quietly. I didn't share my plan with anyone on the Rio Yarapa. I just gleaned everything I could from the talk.

I would summarize it this way: The young boys are lured in with promises. A bit of money and drugs as bait to keep them on the line, but the big bucks and women come when they sell the booty—but not for the boys. The girls are lured in with money and possibly drugs, and a better future (which never comes). Of course, there is a lot of *aguardiente* (rum) involved. When the narcos have enough booty accumulated and the coast is clear, they disappear into the night to meet a bigger boat and transfer their dope. They receive their pittance, and the wheels of the bus go round and round.

I noticed there were some new clothes on the teenagers and a lot of tipsy young people, so enough was enough. Remember that I had a group of middle schoolers coming in a little while, and we always visited the pueblo. The kids loved to buy souvenirs from the artisans: woven baskets, carved animals, paddles, necklaces. You name it, and there it was. I knew that I had to get moving.

• • •

When I arrived in Iquitos on Friday, I met with the general and all parties involved. We even alerted our powerful friends in Lima to give it extra panache. I gave the coordinates, hints on the lay of the land, and washed my hands and mind of the whole thing. I was going back to the lodge on Monday that week, and I would be returning to the asphalt jungle—better known as Iquitos—on Friday. I decided to put it out of my mind and concentrate on the CET group.

Preparations were always overwhelming for the big groups. This one was fifty-six guests. The first group of the season. We usually had six to eight groups from the first part of June through mid-August. One group the year before was seventy-six guests. That was our limit, bulging at the seams. Normal groups were from twenty-five to forty-five. The bigger the group, the more food we had to transport 110 miles up the Amazon River, so I had plenty to keep me busy. No problem there.

In the two weeks that the narcos had controlled Alicia's house, I passed by at least eight times, maybe more, arriving from Iquitos, going to Puerto Miguel, coming back to the lodge, and going back to Iquitos. I never saw anything fishy or weird. I believe that they had all their activity happening behind the house in the jungle.

That is what I passed on to the general. I thought they had to come in from both rivers, the Yarapa and the Ucayali. The Ucayali side would be tricky. They had to go over land for at least seven minutes and there would be a very good chance that the narcos would have sentries in the forest. Oh well. It was what it was.

All this time Alicia was staying at the lodge. We were taking her kids to Puerto Miguel every morning for school, picking workers up, and bringing them back in the afternoon when we took the workers home. It worked out okay, and it kept the kids safe and busy.

Friday finally presented itself, and at noontime I was out of there. As we passed by my neighbor's house I looked out, and for the first time I saw a grungy-looking bearded man with an AK-47. He was crouching by the side of the porch, holding the gun barrel up. We locked eyes for no more than a second, but that was enough to send a chill up my spine and raise the hairs on the back of my neck. I had been made. I placed my hand on the butt of my pistol, even though I knew my chromed .38 would be no equalizer for the AK. I just turned away, not wanting to see if he lowered the muzzle. We were going fast enough, though, and were past the house in seconds. Thank you, my 200-HP Johnson motor.

I usually read on the commute, it being around three and a half hours and all, but that day I was not able to keep the look in that

# CHASING THE DREAM

dirtbag's eyes out of my mind. It was feral in nature, but I got the feeling that I had surprised him. Shit, man, maybe he was taking a dump. LOL, haha.

I got over it. We arrived in the asphalt jungle about 3:45, and I decided it was time for a beer and a smoke at Ari's. Pilsen, a good lager beer, was served up, ice cold, and I rolled one of my famous "black beauties": Captain Black pipe tobacco in a dark brown Rizla rolling paper (you could still smoke in all buildings back then). I took a long draw on the beer, leaned back, enjoying the scent of my ciggy, and noticed my alphabet friend across the way. He looked over, gave a thumbs up, smiled and winked as he got up. He passed by me on his way out, gave me a fist bump to the shoulder, and exited the establishment. I guessed that meant all was well in our kingdom.

I finished my beer, had another, finished my hand-rolled, and went home. I didn't need to be in the office until morning, so I figured I could say hi to the family. Hi, Family! Carmen wasn't home, so I took a shower to wash away the dust, sweat, and my thoughts…my evil thoughts?

# TWENTY

**I SLEPT LIKE A BABY:** waking up frustrated, sleeping, dreaming violently, waking up, et cetera. Carmen was sawing logs, so I finally just slipped into the kitchen and watched the sky change from black to grey to rosy-blue. Then I made my special espresso and greeted a brand new day.

I really didn't know how to greet the day: like one of my last, or a new beginning? I knew that if I went out to the lodge on Monday I may not be returning alive on Friday, now that one of the narcos had been seen and had identified me.

On the other hand, if the raid were to happen sometime on the weekend it would all be over, and I would not have to be burdened with it anymore.

Do you think it was evil to hope? Hope that the raid would happen? People could get hurt, maimed, or killed. But-and I really mean but-they were doing something illegal, immoral, and detrimental to everyone. After all, they had commandeered my neighbor's house, and if there was one thing I really couldn't stand, it was bullies.

As a matter of fact, as I think back to my first real confrontation

## CHASING THE DREAM

with a bully, I believe now that the powers to be were by my side that day and stayed with me forever.

I was about eight or nine at the time, and my older sister Tanya (my elder by two years) and I were in the same elementary school way out in the country. We rode the bus together to and from school. I was rough, popular, but wimpy in size (coffee and cigarettes do that to kids). Tanya was developed for her age and very cute. You know how kids are: do bad things to get attention, especially for the opposite sex.

There was this boy in her class named Billy. Billy was big for his age (future football star) and really pushy. I think he was attracted to my sister, but she wasn't giving him the time of day. Day by day he seemed to get more abusive to the other students on the bus, pushing and saying derogatory things. Tanya and I sat together—but not always. One day "Billy the Bully," as he was called behind his back, got a feather up his ass. He confronted her, kind of like crowding her, and when she told him to leave her alone, it looked to me like he shoved her and called her a bitch.

Well, I really don't know what came over me, but I was out of my seat and on his ass before he could react. He was about a foot and a half taller than me, so plan B kicked in. I attacked below the ribcage, in the organs, and farther below too. He went down, and I kicked at him until he fell out of the bus.

Believe it or don't, he didn't reciprocate later, nor did he pick on smaller kids on the bus, and he never looked me in the eye again. I did get in a bit of trouble in the principal's office. I'll never forget those damned wooden paddles with the holes drilled in them.

Enough meandering; back to the punks.

I decided to just sit on pins and needles and wait to see how it all came down. I went to my office and talked with Don Teddy on our UHF communication radio. All was quiet, A-okay. Hmmm. I went about my business, reviewing the food inventory, signing checks, sending one of my office assistants to the bank for cash, creating a new food inventory for the week (I had about thirty-five workers to feed at the lodge), and I tried to ignore the pins and needles in my butt cheeks.

End of day, no relief in sight, I saddled up my Yamaha dirt bike and sped off to my home. Carmen and Naylita were there, and we decided to go for a walk after dinner. We liked to walk the broken sidewalks around our neighborhood. We could talk, laugh, and stop for a D'Onofrio ice cream. Little Nayla loved that.

Sunday morning, the sun was up, cocks were crowing (in more ways than one), and a new day dawned. I had to go to the office to talk to Don Teddy, for we had only two times a day to communicate by radio. When groups were at the lodge we talked three times every day, and the radio was left on at the office for emergencies.

Coffee, breakfast, and looking at these beautiful girls made everything right. We hung for a while, and I began to feel the pins and needles again. Fifteen minutes until talk time, so I kissed Carmen and Naylita, kick-started my bike, and roared off into the mayhem of Iquitos: horns honking, people yelling, exhaust stifling. What more could you want in a living environment?

I unlocked the office door, rushed over to switch on the radio, and Don Teddy was already yelling, "*Cinco-cero, Cinco-cero. Cinco-cero, Cinco-cero!*" (Our special call: five-zero, five-zero). Over and over.

I grabbed the handheld transmitter and responded, "*Adelante Cinco-cero.*"

"Sr. Norman, *buenos dias.*"

"Buenos dias, Don Teddy, *que novedades?*" (What's up?)

I will convey this conversation in English.

He began, very agitated and excited: "In the middle of last night, the sky lit up like it was the day. Very loud roars and the sound of

# CHASING THE DREAM

gunfire were all around Alicia's house. This lasted for a very long time, and it felt like Armageddon. Men yelling, women screaming, and the sound of a helicopter obliterated everything. There was nothing but noise. After a while there was only a gunshot now and then, no loud voices. Then the big lights went out and there was nothing but darkness and flashlight beams coming from the house of Alicia. I walked to the dock and tried to see if there was anything going on. There was a lot of commotion, figures moving around in the dark, but there was not enough light for me to see who they were. In one flashlight beam I saw a patch of camo uniform, and I heard a few static crackling radio transmissions, but I believe that everyone was moving toward the Ucayali River, probably moving the booty to boats."

I asked, "Is it over now?"

"I can't really tell," he said. "I will take a canoe and go past the house to see if everything is over."

"Okay, I will wait here for your transmission. Over and out."

I sat there struggling with my demons. Gratification, guilt, thankfulness, regret, and all the other bullshit balances a consciousness makes to justify its equilibrium. I finally came up with my way to deal with it: FUCK IT! I did what I did, and I cannot let it bother me… Cold? I don't think so.

Thirty minutes later Don Teddy was transmitting again, "Cincocero, Cinco-cero!"

Back at ya, "Adelante, Cinco-cero."

"Sr. Norman, there is nothing and no one there. Everything is trampled—her corn, yuca, and tomatoes—there is just a big hole in the jungle behind her house and trash everywhere. The smell of gunpowder is still heavy, but I don't see any blood. I believe some of them escaped into the jungle."

"Okay, take a few workers and clean up the mess so when Alicia goes back it looks a little better and her kids aren't traumatized. Fill in the hole too."

"*Afirmativo*, Sr. Norman."

I guessed that it was time for me to go for a beer and a cig. I had to think of the ramifications imposed upon me now. Why did that dirtbag asshole have to lock eyes with me and engrave me in his memory? That could potentially be a future problem for me if he was alive and had escaped.

We moved Alicia and her kids back into her house, helped her get settled, and bid her well. She would have to plant new crops, wait for them to grow, and suffer for a while. I told her that we would help with all we could. The group coming to the lodge would supply rice, beans, and other food left over from the meals. We had groups coming for eight straight weeks, so she shouldn't be too bad off.

I had my guys glean information from the village, and it seems that Don Teddy was right. Most of the real narcos got away by running off into the jungle. Most of the ones captured were the young boys and girls from the villages. The only two that were worth the effort, real narcos, were drunk. The booty was what made all the difference in the world. The police got all of it, a little over a ton, some money, and a few guns.

Not one of my Alphabet Agency acquaintances or the general ever mentioned anything about the raid, and of course I wasn't even involved, right? Goodnight, Irene!

It seemed to me that nothing had really happened. Alicia was back in her house, the CET groups came and went, our weekly craft fair was a raging success, all our employees were eating too much and looking pudgy—or prosperous, whichever way you wanted to look at it. I was still traveling to the lodge every week, Carmen accompanying me once in a while, and when there weren't tourists we would sometimes make it a family affair, with all the kids swimming in the river, laughing, eating, visiting Puerto Miguel, and doing what people do in the Amazon jungle.

When the high season ended and I was back to traveling to the lodge solo again for a couple of months, I began noticing a strange speedboat cutting in behind us around the pueblo of Esperanza (about halfway to the lodge). The boat followed us for about thirty minutes, 150 yards back, turned around, and disappeared into a creek.

Five days later on our way back to the concrete jungle the same boat cut into the river behind us again. Déjà vu! It followed the same program but reversed. I am not a paranoid person, but it did seem strange.

Two days later I traveled to the lodge again. When we were coming close to Esperanza, I told my boat driver to hug the bank of the river around twenty feet out and slow down to twenty knots. As we passed I saw the boat nestled into a small overgrown creek. Same boat. I looked through my binoculars, and there were four bearded men in old fatigue pants and dirty T-shirts…wait a minute, were those gun barrels that I saw? They weren't paying attention because of my trick, so they didn't see me looking at them.

Now, there is an aguardiente (90% sugarcane rum) distillery in Esperanza. We pulled to the bank, stopped, and disembarked like we were going to the distillery. This was something I did quite often to show the tourists how rum was made from the sugar cane. It is really cool.

Out of the corner of my eye I could see the bow of the speedboat barely visible in the mouth of the creek. I bought a few bottles of the rum, and we embarked on our way again. When we had our lead, the speedboat pulled out and repeated the same program as before.

Was this trying to intimidate me? Good luck, boys! Five days later, it was a rerun.

When I got back to Iquitos, I made an appointment with the general. We had a coffee, talked a bit, and then I told him the story. It all sounded so strange, but it could turn into something bad quickly. The general was thinking of a possible kidnapping for money or revenge.

There was a floating dock near the area of Aguajal, upriver from Esperanza, where the anti-drug police had their checkpoint for all boats. These police had two camo speedboats with 50-caliber machine guns bolted to the bow. Ominous! He had a plan. I liked the plan. It would work.

I had a nice two days with Carmen; we went dancing on Sunday at Las Camelias and watched some movies in the evening. Monday midday I would find out if the general's plan would work.

Monday morning. Humid and muggy as always, and I prepared for my weekly trip. I was very fortunate that there were no tourists in these weeks. The plan would not work if there were tourists in my boat. Too much risk. I left at 10:30 in the morning; the river was flat and the sky was a beautiful Columbia blue. When you traveled on the Amazon River you could never predict how your journey would turn out. That day was like driving on a freshly paved street in the U.S. There was not a ripple on the water's surface. My boat skimmed the surface, planing on the keel, at approximately fifty miles per hour. I used less gas when the river was like that, a good thing.

When we were two kilometers from Esperanza, I saw the two camo boats by the bank. They were enclosed with bulletproof glass, so I couldn't see much, but the long-barrel guns were very visible. We sped by, and I knew that they knew who they were looking for...me! This very distinctive boat named *Yacuruna*, "the father of the water."

When we were about to arrive at the speedboat's hiding place, I

## CHASING THE DREAM

saw two police gunboats leave the bank, speeding toward us. By the time we passed the hidden creek and were near Esperanza, I saw the speedboat leave the creek and begin their program of tailing me. They had no idea what was about to happen. The general told me to keep the pedal to the metal and do not look back. Eleodoro, my driver, moved the throttle all the way forward and pushed the boat to sixty…full!

I just had to look back. All I could see was the speedboat cranking to its port into the middle of the river, trying to escape the gunboats, which were about 100 yards behind it, closing rapidly. Figures in the police boats were manning the guns, and white water was spraying everywhere. I turned back around, looking forward, and took a sip of the firewater I had purchased the week before.

I arrived at the lodge in one piece, had lunch, drank a beer, and rolled one of my "black beauties." Five days later I returned to Iquitos without an occurrence, and never was bothered again. Thank you, General, you are a gentleman and a scholar.

**PART 13**

# WE'RE ON OUR WAY TO NOWHERE

*California, heading toward ??*
*Early summer 1971*

# TWENTY-ONE

**REMEMBER, THE THREE OF US**—Larry, Rita, and I—were piling into an old Rambler station wagon with everything we owned (in those days it wasn't much) and taking off to be back-to-the-land-ers. Driving was something we all knew how to do, so we figured we could drive nonstop to where we ended up, and we did. It took us a while to chart out the course. The fastest route to the Midwest was Interstate 80. Once we got there we could decide where we wanted to search for land. The only place to be in the wilderness was in the foothills of the mountains, Appalachia. I guess we were just letting the car drive us. Larry had lived in West Virginia when he was young, before moving to Goshen, Indiana. He told us how beautiful and green it was.

We meandered southeast through Ohio, into West Virginia, and traveled through Cairo (Egypt was a bit out of our way, but what the hell!) and on to Harrisville. This is where it got a bit strange for us. We were long-haired, bearded, strangely dressed young people wanting gasoline, food, and other supplies. I know all these dueling banjo residents staring at us were thinking, "There goes the neighborhood!"

There wasn't much vegetarian/natural foodstuffs to choose from, because every single thing was refined and white. Oh well, we did have dried food still from the Amish in Indiana. There had to be a health food store somewhere. If not, we would have to order it all from Walnut Acres in Pennsylvania. Hippy gotta do what a hippy gotta do! We'd make it work.

We headed south on smaller and smaller roads, looking for "For Sale" signs. No such luck. Up came a town sign for Mahone, so I suggested that we ask there. As we came around the curving mountain road there were two buildings, one on each side of the road. We pulled into the Mahone General Store and entered.

There was a man behind the counter reading the Harrisville paper. He looked up and asked, "What y'all lookin' fer?" He looked us over and continued, "Y'all's not from 'round here, are ya?"

We three looked at each other, and Larry asked if he knew anyone selling land.

"Where ya' from?"

"California," I said. "We are looking to buy some land, build a few structures, grow food, and live naturally."

You know, in those days I really believed that you ran into the people you were meant to connect with.

Mac was his name, and his wife was Gerta. She came in to view the spectacle, and I didn't see any judgment, disgust, or deceit in their eyes.

"I own most of the land around here, but I don't think I want to sell any," he said. "This land has been in my family from the beginning, and it goes back beyond the Plum Run," he said, pointing with his thumb behind his back.

We were wheedling him, and he was turning out to be a cool guy. He sort of looked like Jabba the Hutt but not fat, just pudgy. He was probably in his mid-sixties at that time and had a sense of humor. We

## CHASING THE DREAM

had nowhere to sleep that night, and the car was too crowded, so he let us stay in his auction house across the road. It was good to be indoors, and we rolled out our fart bags on the wooden floor, ate some hippy kibble (granola), and crashed.

When I awoke in the morning, I looked around a bit and saw a post office sign on the front of the general store. Old Mac was the Postmaster of Mahone, West Virginia: population 13, or something like that. I'll bet he was the mayor too. We started in on him first thing, and by midday he had agreed to sell us three acres at the corner of his property way back in the forest. He knew a surveyor who would be willing to do the work at our expense to find the colonial-era brass corner markers and plot the land for us to purchase. Mac would draw up the document, and we would register it in the Harrisville Courthouse.

We were so happy, pigs in shit all the way.

We drove down to the bottom of the holler, parked at our only neighbor's shack, continued walking across the flat and then up the road to the wild and wooly forest we were buying, with the surveyor and his equipment. We agreed to be his helpers because he was giving us a good deal. He definitely earned his bucks, but he was an incredibly astute man. He laid the plot map on a rock; it looked like it had seen a lot of better days—it was almost brown, and hand-drawn. He found the corner markers using his compass and dividers for the direction and distances, dug around in the forest litter and uncovered brass markers that were ancient.

We just measured the three acres out; he drove new markers in the ground and indicated trees on the map to show line-of-sight location. He made a new map for the purchase docs, registered the sale, money changed hands, and we were the new owners of wilderness land in good old West Virginia. What was that old saying? "What you don't know can't hurt you." Hmmm, sure it can; it can kill you, and it almost did.

# TWENTY-TWO

**WE DID IT!** We spent a few nights in Mac and Gerta's auction house while we were building our *wickiup* (a Native American shelter of bent branches covered with pine boughs and other leafy branches).

We did cheat a little bit. We covered it with a waxed cloth tarp to help keep us dry. Then we applied the pine boughs and other branches. We lived, cooked, slept, cried, laughed, and dreamt of being a bit more comfortable. We were sleeping in our bags on beds of pine boughs. We did order food from Walnut Acres through the Mahone Post Office. Turnaround time was bad, but when the food arrived we were truly thankful.

*Norman with his D-35 in front of wickiup framing*

## CHASING THE DREAM

Big problem: water. At first we carried water down from Mac's store. Water wasn't sold like it is today. We had to buy distilled water for irons and batteries and use those containers for drinking water. Rita was crying a lot, but there was nothing we could do. Our relationship fell by the wayside, and she was sad much of the time. We were existing like settlers a hundred years ago, but straddling the fence just enough to remember how it was before.

Then we met Greazer and our lives changed. He lived in a small shack above us. He had lived there all his life. His parents raised him on the side of this mountain. He was the epitome of everything you've heard about backwoods people. Clarence Bickerstaff was his name, and he ate only Vienna sausage in the tin. His yard had thousands of empty tins in piles here and there. He wore black boots, black pants, a dress shirt, a vest, and a black hat. Every part of his ensemble was worse for wear, but he must have had a few of everything because nothing was deathly dirty. Oh, that's right, he had a long grey beard too.

We actually became friends with him, and he showed and taught us many things. One day when we were walking, he told us that his father had hand-dug a water well a ways up from our land. I asked him if he remembered where it was. Well, of course he did, for he had to carry the water to their house. Larry and I brought a shovel and buckets—off we went. Up the mountain road and into the forest a ways, he stopped and looked at the trees and the ground. He walked forward, knelt down, and began pushing the litter around.

Voila! He freed a rotting wooden cover with rusted tin nailed on the top side, lifted it off, and there was a lot of debris inside the hole. "You have to dig down about three to four feet. Get all that debris out. See, you can tell that everything is wet and soupy. By golly, I believe it still can be used! This water was sweet and fresh. Some of the wells have oil in them and are fouled. Let's get 'er cleaned out and see what kinda water comes in."

The well was a hole about sixteen inches in diameter; hard sand and clay kept it from caving in. The water that seeped in was sweet and very clear. Greazer said it was fed by an underground spring. Better than our bottled water today. We filled our four buckets, and Larry and I began sloshing water around while Greazer carried the shovel. The buckets were half full by the time we arrived home. Rita was surprised, and even smiled. That was nice to see.

Greazer also showed us how to find wild ginseng. He said that it hid from you, and you had to have a special eye to capture it. Larry actually got pretty good at spotting it and harvested a small amount.

I know you have been thinking, "Where and when do they wash their bodies? Yuck!" We had a mountain stream, called a "crick," down a small hill. It was cold and clean—not really for drinking, though; we'd probably end up getting "beaver fever," also known as giardia. Every evening before dark we bathed with Dr. Bronner's peppermint soap. That really got a body going.

Rita wasn't adapting to the hardships we all faced. Larry and I had gone through life-and-death situations, had weathered many a storm, pushed onward against all odds, and made it. This truly was a very difficult task that we were attempting. We really couldn't expect her to put up with our death wish (as some people called it). So we talked it out, and we came to the conclusion that she would go back to New York and be able to live a normal life. We would drive her there, deposit her at her parents' house, drive back to Mahone, and continue preparing for winter. We had to have cabins built by the end of September, and it was July. Maybe when we were finished she would want to be part of the adventure again.

We had no electricity, no power tools, no chainsaws, so every tree was cut by crosscut saw, Larry on one side and me on the other.

# CHASING THE DREAM

Back and forth, back and forth. Down goes the tree, and it was cut into sections to use for the cabins. It was a slow process compared to what we were used to, but we were trying to turn our backs on the hustle and bustle—trading it for a simpler life.

Our cabins were getting to the stage of almost habitable. I guess that is why evolution and progression happen in the human organism. To make life easier, maybe?

We had built a small shed to store tools and were still living in the leaking wickiup. We were racing against the coming winter, slaving to be able to have a warm, dry place to spend the winter. We almost made it, but not quite.

First of all, our food stock was running low, and therefore we were adding wild things to our diet. In California I had harvested a variety of wild greens and mushrooms as they came into season. So I was very surprised when we came across a large display of chanterelle fungus near a tree. Beautifully funnel-shaped edibles. I took a small piece, smelled it, and popped it in my mouth. The true test. Nothing happened, and the next day we harvested quite a few, cooking them into a soup. It was pretty damned good. Darkness came, our fire burned down, and we turned in.

I don't know what time it was, but it was a new moon and darker than hell when I jerked awake and barely got my head out the side of the wickiup…retching and retching. Everything I had eaten was coming up. The only pain that I could remember (in this life) that was as bad was the appendicitis I experienced at sixteen. It didn't stop there. It was like I could see in the dark.

I slipped out of my fart bag, started crawling toward the light, running head-on into a wall. Wait a second; it was night, not day, and so I felt around. I was still inside the wickiup. I had to be hallucinating, but not just that. There was a whole different reality being played out in front of my eyes. I felt my way around the wall until there was an opening. I slid through and crawled forward, retching again and again. I'm not really sure how long this went on, but the pain was intense, and the dry heaving was obnoxious and hurt even more. After a while I just lay on my back until I thought I had died…nothing but black.

The sun peeking through the trees woke me up. I lifted one eyelid to test the scene, and everything appeared to be physical—you know, like the Earth. I felt okay, but my stomach muscles were sore and I was very, very thirsty with a headache. I then realized that I had been on the bare ground all night outside. I looked around, wondering where Larry was, and saw him about ten feet away, sprawled with his arms flung to the sides, looking dead. I forced myself to stand up, maybe not such a good idea, and stumbled to his side. His hair and shirt were crusted with dried gunk, so I tentatively looked at the front of me and realized that we were in the same boat—crusty crabs.

I touched him and found that he was warm and had a pulse. He was coming around also, so I guess we had taken the same dark journey, just different trails. While Larry was coming to I stumbled over to our freshwater container and pulled some long hard drinks. I filled a cup and took it over to him. My mouth tasted like cockroaches had crawled inside and died—a week ago.

I grabbed the Doc Bronner's and made my way down the hill to the "crick," lay down in a small water-filled depression, and relished the cold water. Larry was making his way down too.

When we were cleaned up and presentable, we made a fire, sat close to warm up, and talked about our near-death experience. We were okay with it. We weren't going to eat any more of those chanterelles, though. The next time we went into Harrisburg, I went to the library and learned that there was one copycat of the beautiful chanterelle: the very poisonous Jack-O-Lantern. I guess that was one of those "what you don't know…" Yup!

# TWENTY-THREE

**WE WERE GAINING ON THE BATTLE,** but it was the ending days of August, and we had already had some summer storms and rain. We were a few weeks away from being snug in the rug for winter when a storm blew in. This is the CliffsNotes summary of what happened to our bodies and minds:

It was a radical northerly storm that started out easy and grew into a wet, windy nightmare. Larry and I were working heartily when the winds began to blow. Larry was trying to get his cabin logs chinked, and I was trying to make sure that the wind wouldn't blow rain into my windmill cabin, for there were a few spaces left from the overlapping split logs. In other words, we were trying to waterproof our cabins with no modern-day products.

The weather was getting blustery and overcast, and the sky began threatening rain. I could smell it in the wind. As the day slowly disappeared and the sky got darker and darker, a light misty rain began. We were still able to work. When the actual drops of water started falling, we scrambled to guard the tools and ran to our cabins. It was really windy by that time, and the rain was blowing sideways at times.

I noticed immediately that some of my corners were leaking, water running down the corner posts when the wind gusted.

I guess Larry was having similar problems with water, so we decided to go back to the wickiup to ride out the storm. We built a small fire as the wind velocity was building outside. I thought I heard and felt the skin of the wickiup moving around. It was almost dark by now, and we thought the storm would blow over soon. We moved a few of our special things into the tool shed, like guitars and books, because it offered the best protection from the rain. We tarped them too, just in case.

As time dragged on, the storm got worse, not dissipating, and the wind grew stronger. Wow, it was a good thing we put that tarp on the wickiup under the pine boughs. We were still pretty dry, except for some drips where the tarp had begun to deteriorate due to age. We were handling it. We actually made some popcorn with cayenne pepper and salt over the fire, which was always our favorite after-dinner snack… now it was dinner. We were trying to stay as calm and as casual as possible, you know—we could handle this!

Then the unthinkable happened: The tarp blew up and ripped in the wind, leaving only about half of the frame covered. We were lucky that part of the covering was facing the wind and we did have some shelter to huddle in so we could work out another plan. I didn't believe the tarp would last much longer. We had to move.

We decided to forget what was in the wickiup, grab our bags and move to the tool shed, which was right next to our shelter. Maybe it was still dry. We did so, throwing the tools out in the rain. We were able to huddle. There wasn't a door on the shed—no need in the wilderness—but the back corner was facing the wind, so we were out of the blowing rain, more or less. I had found our little flashlight, but the batteries weren't fresh so it wasn't very bright.

## **CHASING THE DREAM**

I remember thinking, "At least now we can relax a bit, the worst could be over." NO WAY!

I felt something on my neck. It really could have been anything: spider, ant, centipede, lizard, or maybe a snake! I grabbed it with my fingers, and it was an ant. Well now, there is no such thing as "an ant," meaning one, is there? I turned on the weak flashlight and shone it around us. It looked like the ants had the same idea as we had: Shelter in the shed. Great minds, right?

I tried to brush them off, but they were all over me. I just gave up, placed my hands over my face, and leaned against my knees. I could overcome, yes I could, and I did.

The storm went on and on. To finish this segment up without you all falling asleep or chewing your fingernails off, however it affects you, the long and the short of it is: Somehow, somewhere, sometime, with some streak of luck we made it up to Mac's store. He let us camp out in his auction house and I confessed, "I have to get out of this shithole."

Larry agreed, we needed something in our lives, right now, different from what we were experiencing. We needed a break! We were leaving for a while.

We went to Indiana for the late fall and winter. My mom was into a Psychic Circle of Friends that Larry and I became part of for a while, meeting a different segment of society. One of the members was an artist, and she owned a blueberry farm. We would pick and eat tons of blueberries that fall.

Larry and I drifted apart somewhat, with me living and working in Mishawaka and Larry in Goshen. We had plans to go back down to West Virginia in the late spring when it warmed up.

• • •

Larry stayed with his parents and hooked up with a girl from Goshen, passing the cold season with her in a teepee. The artist friend of my mother's let them erect the teepee in her blueberry orchard and live until spring, Native American style.

*Larry and Victoria by their teepee in the snow*

I stayed with my mom and worked the cold season as a mortar-mixing hod carrier for a brick mason. I mixed his mortar, carrying it and the bricks to the second floor for him to lay the bricks in a bed of mortar. We still worked when the thermometer sunk to the twenties, but when it dipped to the teens it was just "too cold to hold," because I couldn't keep the mortar from turning to slushies.

Our spring plans got fuzzier and fuzzier for me. I lamented about my musical aspirations and how I wanted to record songs again. I guess I have always been torn between the soil and my aspirations. I grew up in the country, and I've grown my food. I also have the need to release creative energy, hence my art and music. I wrote a song in the late '60s, a mix of the two: earth and spirit.

### MIDWESTERN FARMER

*He is a Midwestern farmer*
*He helps grow the corn for this land*
*His woman she is a lady*
*Doing the best that she can.*

It goes on and on, but I won't bore you. I am just trying to say, "Larry, I am not going back to West Virginia in the spring. I am going back to California to form a band, play clubs again, and record my songs. Now that you have Victoria you won't be lonely, so I will contact you if I ever decide to come back. My very best of luck to you, my brother, and your future family. 1972, OM TAO."

PART 14
# BUILDING A LIFE IN PERU

*Yacumama Lodge and The Concrete Jungle
1999 – August 2001*

# TWENTY-FOUR

**NOW THAT WE WERE** in the groove with tourists, good employees, and a future to look forward to, Carmen and I decided it was time to buy or build a house with some of the comforts that she had experienced and that I was used to in my country. I had no intentions of returning, and Carmen had no thoughts of going to the U.S. other than to visit my family.

So in the off season we started looking around the better neighborhoods for a good deal. We found one across the sidewalk from where we were renting. A lawyer I had used a few years before was selling his second house in our project. A pretty good deal and a great location: a corner lot, which meant more windows and more light in the house.

I made a deal with him, went to my bank, took out a home loan, pulled a mortgage—*hipoteca*—and closed the deal.

Now was the part I liked the most: the design, the drawings, and the engineering. We would start as soon as I received my demo permit. We asked around and found a house builder. Of course he had never built anything like the house that I had in mind, but it was okay because I was going to be the boss anyway. I found an architectural draftsman to do the drawings, a local who meditated, followed Eastern religious practices, and was considered a weirdo by the neighborhood. That was okay by me.

The first thing I did was demolish the whole back of the house and start over.

*Demo*

*Start-up*

*House profile*

*My original drawing*

*Finished product: our house picket fence and all*

## CHASING THE DREAM

I designed and built this house to replicate a ship. "Come sail away, come sail away, come sail away with me!"

Y2K came and went with not so much as a ripple. The Green-Tracks group was there with Bill Lamar, rocking on New Year's Eve. I finished the house in mid-2000, and Steve Shephard (the white water man) brought a group to the lodge shortly thereafter. When we returned to Iquitos, on their way home he visited us in this house with his "to be" wife Jeanie. We had some CET groups over the summer, RHP medical groups throughout the year, and various Free Independents.

By the end of 2000, Carmen was pregnant: We had a baby in the oven. That was damn cool. Everything seemed pretty secure. We were living in our new house, and I even had doors on all the rooms, the bathrooms and kitchen tiled, and protective bars everywhere they were needed. I wasn't about to have another break-and-enter episode. We were starting to feel like real people again.

• • •

You always have to watch out for the feeling of security. In the midst of all these good times, I had to find out my trusted employee Pablo was robbing me. Yes, the one who started out as my house boy in 1993, went to accounting school, and moved up to office helper, then became my office assistant, then co-manager with my brother-in-law Jorge, and then, embezzler. In every way he could he skimmed money, from purchasing food for the tourists to falsifying receipts. I was so busy with tourists, I gave orders and payments, and they carried everything out. Yup, sure did!

I was crushed and could have pressed charges. I mean, it was grand-grand larceny, countless thousands of soles (the Peruvian currency). But where would it have gotten me? He had spent the money. I could have sent him to jail…but fuck it! I had been to kangaroo court so many times, five to be exact, that I was getting tired of the banana republic judicial system. I was going to try to put more controls, checks and balances, on everything that I did to try to minimize thievery. Good fuckin' luck, Normando!

I started 2001 with just one person in the office when I was out at the lodge with tourists. That was real good checks and balances, wasn't it? There was nothing I could do. Every one of my gringo helpers had crashed and burned in Peru. I was alone, like always, running a very difficult business in a South American country by myself. I never really signed up for this service. I was supposed to be walking around in a pith helmet with a riding crop, directing workers to do my bidding!

I could feel that everything was kind of disintegrating in Miami. Tourists that arrived told me that they had problems booking, they couldn't understand the agent at Eco Expeditions, and didn't get call-backs. A few booked through other agencies. There were problems everywhere, but we did have bookings, and I would receive and serve them.

RHP Medical came in February, and we lived through the spring, but we only had one CET group. I was told that they were having a few problems, and Jim Cronk was bringing one group from Castine, Maine, to the lodge. Okay, we were on it.

I guess the group was Jim's, because he was the only person who came with them. Since they had pen-pal letters, school supplies for the kids and the school, Carmen said she would help (six months pregnant).

This was one of the best, most fun, and interested groups we ever had. It was small but very rewarding. This group was our last group of 2001. We continued to welcome ecotourists for the rest of the high season, and Carmen continued to swell. It was looking like our new daughter, Stacy Ann, was going to be a bit late.

## CHASING THE DREAM

*CET Group, Castine, Maine
(My little buddy up there)*

*Carmen with pen pals*

Patty's medical group was at the lodge. It was the second week of August and also the second week of the group's stay at the lodge. I received a radio transmission in the morning on Saturday, August 11, 2001, saying that I had better come home, now! I prepared the lodge and the group for my absence, jumped in the *Yacuruna*, and sped off for Iquitos.

I rushed home, and Carmen was having the uncomfortable feeling that the time was drawing nigh. We went for her last examination on Sunday morning, August 12, 2001. The doctor examined her, said she wasn't quite ready, and sent us home. A half an hour later I was playing my guitar for her, and I noticed that she kept closing her eyes and grimacing. I timed the pain and deemed that she was having contractions close enough together to actually have the baby.

We hailed a motocar and jetted over to the Clinica Ana Stahl, where we were going to admit her for the delivery. When we arrived Carmen was weak and feeling very faint. I got her into a room as fast as possible. The nurse checked her heartbeat and the baby's. The baby was in distress; they saw that Carmen was fully dilated for giving birth. They couldn't get any of the monitors to work, so the nurse tried to set up an IV with dilator. Carmen told them no, she was having the baby, and they rushed her to the delivery room.

She should never have been sent home an hour before by the ob-gyn. When we got to the delivery room, he came rushing in dressed in street clothes; he had been playing futbol. The nurse was trying to put a hospital gown over his shirt but was having a hard time. I was sitting front and center and saw everything. I noticed that the pediatrician ran in, giving the ob-gyn a very dark look.

I had delivered both of my older children in our home, and I knew what a natural, normal birth looked like. This was not normal; they had waited too long. The meconium had been released in the womb, and

## CHASING THE DREAM

Stacy had aspirated it. She popped out and was handed to the pediatrician, not breathing. Carmen noticed the look on my face and was very distraught. He slapped Stacy on the butt, and there was no response, nothing. He tried again…nothing.

He placed her on the table and massaged her heart. She moved, then went limp again and peed. He had a very small, very old vacuum machine on the table, with a soft clear tube attached to it. He turned it on and began feeding it through her mouth to her lungs. I could see the meconium and amniotic fluid being pulled out of her lungs, and he massaged her heart again. She came to and moved her arms up, then went limp again. He continued to suck the liquid from her lungs and massage her chest (as long as he was massaging her heart, it was pumping her blood). He continued to suck and massage, and she came to again, moved her limbs, and made a strange sound…and then went limp again.

Holy shit, this guy was a miracle worker. The stuff was still coming up the tube, and he was still massaging her little heart, over and over and over. All of a sudden she came to and started to cry, not hysterically, but kind of like whimpering. I noticed that there was no more liquid being sucked up the tube, and he pulled it out of her throat. He barked at the nurse (frozen in place) to give him a blanket for her; she complied quickly.

Stacy's temperature had dropped radically, and she was at risk of hypothermia. He wrapped her up and held her for a few seconds, almost like he was saying a prayer. Then he handed her to the nurse and barked another order: "Get her in the incubator!" All this time, Carmen was just lying there with everyone frozen around her. She had been released from the stirrups and covered up, and was ready to be cleaned up and moved to her room. I gave her a kiss on the forehead and was escorted out.

Well now, that was a pretty radical birth. I told them to let me know immediately when she was settled and I could see her. Carmen was delivered to her room, and we looked at each other. I could tell that we felt the same emotions.

We almost lost her; she actually died three times from the negligence of one doctor, and she was saved by the intelligence and skill of another: Dr. Caira. He was her pediatrician for the rest of our time in Peru. He was our hero, and we praised his efforts to everyone.

I had to fight all the way to get in to see Stacy in the incubator. I finally forced myself in and they left me alone. I talked to her, took her hand, and she moved her head, facing me. Of course she recognized my voice, nine months of listening to me in the womb. I made them let Carmen in to feed her, because they didn't want her to do that either. What? The baby's first drink of nourishment should be her mother's milk. Am I right or wrong?

Stacy is a strange child, adept and aware. Truly a millennial, but pretty much "on top of it." I remember when Carmen asked her why she picked her as her mother, and us as her parents. She said, "I heard Dad's voice first, and I moved toward that sound." That makes me remember the day when she was three or four years old and Carmen and I were talking about my Aunt Betty in the dining room. Stacy was playing with her "Little People" stuff in the Florida room. (My Aunt Betty, second mom and a very kindred spirit, had passed on years before.)

We were talking about some occurrence in my life, and I loudly spouted my aunt's name, "Aunt Betty." Stacy retorted, "What!" from the Florida room.

Kinda' weird!

Anyway, back in Peru, we finally were able to get them both discharged and home. I had constructed all of her nursery furniture, and we were ready for the baby onslaught! The next thing was to travel to the U.S. to see my mom and family. I made flight reservations for September 10, 2001. We were so excited to show off our new daughter, Stacy Ann.

**PART 15**

# HIPPY GOTTA DO WHAT A HIPPY GOTTA DO

*Off to California and Hawaii
December 1971-1981*

# TWENTY-FIVE

**I DRESSED IN A DARK GREY** hooded monk's robe. Packed my bag and said goodbye, hugged and kissed my mom and sister. I had already spoken with Thayer. I was going to help her, help me, and watch over Frog Holler.

To conserve my money I decided to ride the Greyhound Bus to Mill Valley, California. Christmas was coming up, and the California winters were much better than Indiana's: rainy but not bitter cold.

Upon arriving in Mill Valley, I helped make rum fruitcakes, wrap presents, and prepare for festivities. Shortly thereafter, I went to the Petaluma ranch and prepared to hang for a while, acting as guardian and getting my music trip together. I advertised in the newspapers, local rags, and posters on poles. Then I waited.

I solicited a bass player, a guitarist, and a drummer. Any other professional musicians on any other instruments were free to call and try out also. We did have a landline at the ranch, so I was able to screen the calls and make appointments for tryouts. I received quite a few inquiries, some warranted and some not.

From five guitarists I picked one, hands down. Jimmy Dillon was the best acoustic guitarist I had heard.

From four bassists I picked Pat Campbell (we called him "Pat Soup"). He was on top of it.

From three drummers I picked one.

Then there was this strange call from a violinist, asking about the type of music we were going to record. I told her that I was a song writer, and I was going to pay them to record with me. My music was not pigeon-holed, but had rock and country flavors. It was then that she told me that her life was classical music; she did not even know who the Beatles were. She was first chair in the Berkeley Symphony Orchestra, but she wanted to learn new types of music, and had seen my ad on the street in Berkeley. You can bet yer bottom dollar I took her, and it was a very good move. We named her "Fiddle Mary" and she tore up the stage. I had started using the name Cloud before Larry and I had left for West Virginia, and since Jimmy and I were the front men, we decided "Wind and Cloud" would be a good name for our group. Jimmy would be Wind.

We practiced at Frog Holler and got tight. Mary had connections upstate in Northern California, Willits to be exact. This is where we met Tommy Heath of "Tommy Tutone" fame—remember the song "867-5309/Jenny"? He was the house band, and they invited us up a few times to perform in the club. That was fun, and in our time off Fiddle Mary and I searched out the Irish pubs. She knew all the old tunes, and we played for Guinness. Not bad.

We eventually recorded at Funky Features in the Haight. Funky Jack, the owner, liked the music and the money. We worked hard and long hours laying the tracks, but it came to a point of exhaustion and unrest amongst the members. Jimmy talked me into taking a little R&R in Hawaii. Maui, that is. Off we went.

We scrounged around for a few days, bought a car, slept on the beach (sand fleas and all), and traveled around the island drumming up interest. We did, and shortly thereafter were entertaining at the hottest spots available: La Familia restaurant, the Silver Sword Inn, Lahaina Yacht Club, and wherever else they wanted us. It was really a great time, but I became distracted one night when a local girl invited us to crash at her house. Wow, that was really unexpected.

*Cloud (me) in Maui*

I got entangled, and the next thing I knew I wanted to spend more time with her than with Jimmy. Well, things change. I got involved, Jimmy and I didn't entertain so much, and one day Jimmy told me it was time to go back and finish the recording.

I looked at him and said, "I'm not going back. I've found a good life here, and I'm going to stay." Crushing! We were buds, though, and he definitely understood. Bye, Jimmy.

I still played some outside concerts and festivals as "Cloud," and it was good, but not like "Wind and Cloud" for me. I prayed that one day we might play together again.

Now let me tell you, I was caught in the web. She was a beauty; she had a year-and-a-half-old daughter and owned a boutique on Front Street next to the Lahaina Yacht Club. Nice Indonesian batik clothing and a small silk-screening operation to print one-color designs on T-shirts. Not a bad setup.

I thought I was on cloud nine, playing at the yacht club, going to the beach, snorkeling to the Cliff House. I mean, what more could a boy want?

Then the shit hit the fan. I was walking down the sidewalk toward the boutique. It was midday, and I was meeting her to go get a bite to eat. Suddenly there was a Hawaiian man standing in front of me, blocking my path. I zigged to the right, and he did too. I zagged to the left, and he did too, so I just stopped and looked at him. He was about my size but a bit more muscular, nice brown skin, black longish hair, a mustache, and white teeth. I just stood there, waiting for him to talk.

"Hey *haole* (whitey), what the fuck you doin'?"

I looked at him, and he looked rough, but I asked, "What are you talking about?"

"You know goddamned well what I'm talking about. My bra (brother, who turned out to be a haole too) is sitting in prison, and here you are with his wife."

"What the hell you talking about?" I queried. "I met her in La Familia, and she invited me to her house."

He told me the whole sordid story. I realize human nature is far from perfect. I am not going to pass the story on, but just let me tell you that she was still married, her husband was in prison, and I was already smitten. Fuck me!

## CHASING THE DREAM

I decided to leave Maui. I was pretty disappointed with what had transpired. And I just wanted to escape. I wrote Larry and told him I was coming back to West Virginia for his and Victoria's marriage ceremony. I was going to stay for a while and was bringing a teepee with me. Oh boy!

I told her I was leaving and she said, "I want to go with you!"

That was definitely the "fly in the ointment." It was going to be winter in few months, and I knew that I could live through it, but with a warm-weather woman and her child? Hey, what can I say? I was smitten! Weakness rules!

We went, she met my family, we were a part of Larry and Victoria's ceremony in West Virginia. She became pregnant, we lived through the winter in a teepee with elk hides to sleep under, saw my good friends Peggy and Dan, ate a shitload of potatoes, built the place up with another building, and realized how irrational I was being. What the hell were we doing here? Living like we were in 1860. There was a world out there that was 1973. Cars were invented, electricity and inside plumbing were created. There was a whole other world awaiting. Why were we turning our backs on it?

Well, I knew why, but I didn't want to accept the fact that I was searching for a balance that I couldn't find and that may have not even existed yet. We drove our vintage 1953 Chevrolet Bel Air back to California, sold it, and went back to Hawaii. We married, had two children on Maui—Luke in 1974 and Star in 1976. I delivered both children at home and we prospered.

Larry and Victoria (now named Prairie because of the song I composed in 1971, "Prairie Rose," soon to be recorded by a very esoteric and longtime friend of mine, Alicia Bay Laurel) moved to Maui, had more kids, and after a few years they moved back to the mainland.

## NORMAN WALTERS

I created Unity Circle of Friends, a natural foods cooperative that boomed from 1975 through 1977, but all things change, and our situation did too. We divorced, I left the co-op, and the Marxists somehow took it over. In 1978 I went to India two times, studied Hinduism and Buddhism, returned and became a sort of outlaw. I guess that can happen when the rug is pulled out from under you.

# TWENTY-SIX

**THE FOLLOWING SEGMENTS** of my life materialized in a strange way. My ex-wife and two children accompanied me on my second visit to India. She was a follower of Baghwan Shree Rajneesh at that time, and I had some stupid-assed ideas that we could get back together if we were united in a common belief as a family. I also paid for the trip.

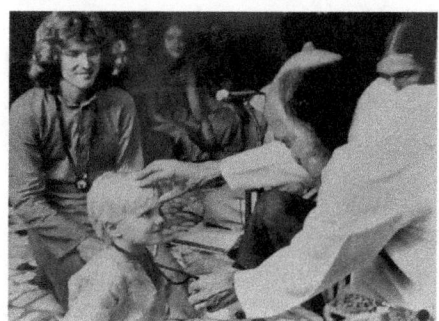 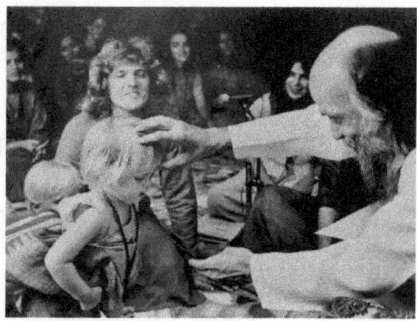

*Myself, Luke, Star, and the Baghwan. Poona, India, 1978*

## NORMAN WALTERS

I had read all of his books and deemed him a very intelligent man (ex-professor of philosophy at a prestigious Indian university) possessing an ability for drawing people searching for a shepherd into his dynasty. He surely had a "golden tongue!" There wasn't room in his ashram for us to stay, so I rented an apartment close by.

At first, there was hope. We cooked our food, attended his talks each morning, had darshan with him, the kids had friends to play with, and it seemed that we were adding building blocks to our family structure. Unfortunately this was not a correct assessment.

For me his talks were good, but I felt a strange magnetic chaos in the gathering room. I started going less and less, taking care of the kids more and more, but the turning point for me was when I saw the AK-47 and the take-down of a "man with a knife" at the morning talk. It was brutal, it was fast, and he was gone! I had heard that Rajneesh had had many attempts on his life, supposedly by the Indian government. He possessed an armada, but this was a bit *extra*. Why would they want him dead?

I do know why—now—and if you are interested, google Rajneesh and read about his escape to the United States, running from Indian tax evasion and fraud. Although it is not clear how he really escaped from India, the most believable version for me was always as a mummy-wrapped "burn victim" with millions of U.S. dollars under his bandages, and his antics in Oregon, ending in his escape, capture, deportation, and demise. An exalted being? If you ask me (twenty-seven Rolls Royces—one ending up in a ditch due to "too much wine" and frolicking—many young concubines, and an expanded view of himself leading to a total snubbing of American laws and criminal justice), he was over the top and ready to crash.

I believe I mentioned this before, but when he was captured the police made a T-shirt that stated: "I BAGGED THE BAGWAN!" with

## CHASING THE DREAM

a likeness of him behind bars. I laughed my ass off about that and sent one to my ex! She didn't share the humor.

Well anyways what I was talking about was the destruction of our relationship in India. As time went on she began going to more and more classes, and I heard words like tantra and intimacy and *WHAT*?

What the hell was going on in these classes? I could only imagine. I asked an acquaintance, and he was totally *down* on these classes. The best thing that he had ever experienced. You got to screw in the classes, learning intimacy and having better orgasms.

That was it for me. I confronted her with it, and she was evasive, but kind of admitted to it. I told her I was leaving, taking the children. I asked if she wanted Star to stay with her. She told me of course she wanted one of them to stay with her. Me, being the dumbest ass in the world, left Star with her mother. I had all the return tickets, and I could have just walked away when she was moaning and groaning in her class, but no, I did what was fair, being human in this world...I only took Luke, and left the return tickets on the table for her and Star.

I will probably never forgive myself for that decision, but please go easy on me. I was "full on" love and peace: do not take advantage of, hurt, or exploit anyone. She was the mother, and she deserved to have her one-and-a-half-year-old daughter with her, who was still nursing. Right?

Wrong, but it took me almost a year to find out the atrocities that had befallen my daughter in India. News was relayed to me by the returning Sanyasins (Rajneesh followers dressed all in orange, with *malas* around their necks, and yes, a picture of him on the mala) about the ashram, because I had been there and they knew my ex and me. The most important ones were the last ones. My daughter was basically living with her *aya* (nanny), *very* sick (my ex was in classes all the time and traveling to Japan to make money), and there had been a get-together at a local hotel, kind of like a pool party. My ex had been distracted, talking to someone, when Star fell in the pool. She was two years old.

Well, nobody noticed at first, then a doctor took notice, dove to the bottom, and brought her up. He performed CPR and brought her back to the living.

When I heard this, I knew it was time to take action. I knew a psychologist friend going to the ashram for a few weeks, so my ex's mother and I halved all of his expenses, so he could bring Star back to me in Hawaii.

Easier said than done. I had to call India, talk to Sheela, "Iron Maiden" at the ashram (Rajneesh's #2), and tell her the story. I advised her that if Star did not come back to the USA with my friend, I would make an international scandal, period! My friend was flying to India in two days, so she told me to call back the next day: Just ask for Sheela.

Those twenty-four hours were forerunners to all the bad twenty-four hours I would ever have in my life.

When I called back, Sheela said, "Bagwan summoned your ex-wife to darshan last night. He convinced her to send your daughter back to the USA with Sri so-and-so, your agent, in one week when he returns to your country." I was very surprised and told her to thank Bagwan and tell him *Shaka Bra* (hang loose).

We gave my friend money for food, hotel, and taxis. He was able to stay, listening to the Buttwan every morning, having darshan, and maybe even contracting amoebic dysentery or botulism at the very least. Just so he made it back with the kid, whatever else happened was his to hold. There was no internet, iPhones, or texting, so I had to wait for an international call to let me know what was happening.

I received the call two days before his projected departure date from India. I had given him documents for Star's travel and more for

# CHASING THE DREAM

the ashram and my ex-wife. Everything was signed and stamped. He and his wife were to pick Star up the morning of the train trip from Poona to Bombay (Mumbai now), flying to Calcutta, Bangkok, Hong Kong, Tokyo, Honolulu, and Kahului, Maui. It was an incredible journey that I owed him for and paid in $$ and kudos. I will always be indebted to my friend for bringing my daughter back to me.

We met at the Kahului airport and I could see that Star was in a confused state. She looked vacant-eyed and numbed to what was happening in her world. I don't think, or I don't want to think, that she was traumatized beyond her ability to adapt.

She looked at me and quickly looked away like she didn't know me. She was in the arms of my friend's wife and had traveled unimaginable miles with them, but then I motioned to let me have her, and I held her close. All the time and distance disappeared, and she was back in her daddy's arms. She relaxed, and I just held her. Memories, synapses, and everything else came back to her. She grabbed my neck and started to cry. I could not control myself and walked with her into the terminal, just feeling the connection again.

My ex-mother-in-law, a friend (beyond time), was very moved and happy that all of our plans had worked out. We worked together to bring her back, and here we were: the culmination of our endeavors in physical form. Star, my baby, was back!

• • •

The next few weeks were difficult, but with the help of her brother and sister, friends, my mother, mother-in-law and a family life again, she slowly came around and normed out—more or less—as you can see by the following photographs:

## NORMAN WALTERS

*Ahhhhhhh!*

# TWENTY-SEVEN

**THERE ARE NO EXCUSES** for my behavior in the next couple of years. I would love to blame my actions and death wishes on outside influences, but that would be copping out.

"I yam what I yam!" This is my story, and I am sticking to it!

Living in the ruins of my life, being a single parent of two wonderfully beautiful children, searching for love in the time of hippy diseases—very difficult—and having no real direction for my cloistered island life, I collapsed into the "dark side," a very real place. I never really believed that I was changing—how could I?—I was searching for direction, and I found it.

It started out innocuously. A lot of my friends were growing these simple little green plants—of course they had to keep them hidden from sight—that were difficult to tend to, but were worth their weight in greenbacks.

I thought to myself, "What harm could it cause, a few beautiful plants?"

Well, I found out just how dangerous it could be in less than sixty days. One of my good hippy friends, Kenneth, came to me one day and was talking about his harvest and all the benefits he had reaped from a very small crop deep in the jungle. We were in his sweat lodge, and I was somewhat interested in his accounting, listening to his words, as I trickled creek water over the steaming rocks.

"The only difficulty was getting nutrients and water to the plants when they were young," he said. "I had to carry two five-gallon containers of water and a backpack full of natural fertilizer for thirty minutes up the mountain through the jungle. I did this every three days for four months, and I harvested fifteen plants. Now I can start building my house.

"How would you like to do a crop with me? With the two of us, we could grow twice the plants and reap twice the rewards. The only difference is that I want to try it on the other side of the island, the West Maui Mountains…Eke Crater."

That volcanic mountain is known to be rife with spirits protecting and warding off unwanted intrusions. I am witness to the truth in these legends…because:

I am meandering now.

Early in the year—1977—Larry, Kenneth, and I were sitting around talking about how we needed an adventure. Something difficult, physically demanding, maybe even a bit fearful. Kenneth had investigated Eke Crater and found that it was just about the most difficult climb, hike, and experience available in the Hawaiian Islands. There—maybe—was a cabin on the top of the crater that we could overnight in. The information noted that not many hikers ever make it to the top due to problems encountered en route: death by falling, heavy wind, hail and rain, and exhaustion. This sounded like just what the doctor ordered.

No permit needed in those days so we made our plans for the big adventure. We parked our car in Wailuku—altitude 294 feet—at

# CHASING THE DREAM

the base of Eke. We started out in jungle-like surroundings, and as we climbed toward the 4,800-foot summit things changed radically. I realized that very soon we would have to pick one of the ridged fingers and follow it all the way to the top since there were no connecting bridges, and their precipice rock faces met 500-plus feet below in the valley.

The closer we got to the deteriorated top of the 1.3 million-year-old crater, the thinner and rockier the ridges became, until we were walking on a path that was no more than eighteen inches wide, the precipice dropping straight down on either side.

The photograph that I am displaying is a rare sight. Eke Crater is normally closed off with clouds and rain.

*Eke Crater on a very rare day*

The early Hawaiians believed that the actual crater was a portal or Heaven's Gate, a doorway between the physical and spiritual worlds. They also believed these spirits or their gods protected the portal.

Anyway, getting back to the story, we did not have a rare beautiful day, we had a socked-in, windy, heavy rainstorm day. Now, the three of us were pretty much die-hards. We were not going to let a little thing like "the weather" hamper our trek. We just pulled our ponchos on and yelled, "*Hele* on!" (Hawaiian for "move on").

As you can see in the photo, there is a plateau at the top, which is the disintegrated cone, turned bog. It is a dangerous place to walk due to the sink holes and lava tubes that *could* lead to the center of the earth. We had been protected from wind all the way up by the pure mass of the mountain itself, but as we crested the top edge, the winds tripled in intensity. I looked back and saw Larry's poncho pulled almost straight up in the air. Kenneth's situation looked even worse… strangling him. I grabbed at my poncho, trying to take up the blousing and bundle it up in my fist. It worked pretty well, but we had to regroup and make a plan. There was no cabin, no shelter, and nowhere to go but back over the edge. We retraced our steps until we could talk, and we hunkered down.

"Holy shit," I yelled, because the noise from the wind was overpowering my voice, sucking it up into the sky. "We've come this far. Is it far enough, or do you want to see the lake?" I looked at the shell-shocked eyes in front of me and realized that mine probably looked the same.

"I want to see the lake," yelled Larry, and Kenneth nodded too.

"Okay, then we need to make a plan. The wind has to be at least seventy-five miles per hour on top, the rain is coming sideways—horizontally—at us, fog is so thick that it is swirling around like banshee hair, and the lake is probably eight hundred to a thousand feet away," I said, adding, "we probably won't even find it, fall down a tube or drown in a sink hole, but are we going?" All three of us smiled and nodded, thumbs up.

That could be one of the dumbest decisions we ever made, but we were there, on a mission to succeed… do or die!

## CHASING THE DREAM

"Now wait a minute," I yelled. "What if one of us gets hurt or disappears in a hole or wanders off?"

"Keep eye contact. Do not lag behind. Let's walk as close to each other as we can," Kenneth said.

"The wind is coming out of the north, which is why it is colder," I said. "It will be hitting us five to seven degrees to our right sides, right in your ear." I looked at Larry.

"Keep your poncho tight around your face. Don't let the wind blow it up and blind you like it did me," he replied. "Crouch down to walk. We only have a third of a mile to go."

"Again," I screamed, "what do we do if one of us disappears?"

Kenneth looked up and exclaimed, "Let's just pray that doesn't happen."

"Then let's get the hell out of here!"

We were better prepared this time as we crested "Hamburger Hill", but the enemy was waiting. The wind and rain were almost full in our face, and it hit us with the force of a freight train. We grabbed hands for the first few yards just to get our bearings, then let go and trudged on. We decided to take turns going first, just to make sure each of us had a chance of a serendipity experience, like falling in a lava tube or disappearing into a sink hole. We wouldn't want to be selfish now, would we?

I took the first shift. I didn't think that it would take us more than fifteen minutes to get to the lake. The bog was almost barren. Very small scrub trees and strange, mossy-looking plants on the ground. The lake was only ten to fifteen feet in diameter, so we could miss it. How could we possibly keep an eye out for it when our eyes were squinting? I could barely see.

My first trip into a sink hole was invigorating. One leg in all the way to the crotch, and my face scrunched into those mossy-looking plants. Now that was fun, especially with the added bonus of my poncho flying up and the rain saturating my back. I didn't lose my shoe... good thing, because those sweet little mossy-looking plants were scratchy and my cheekbone was raw. Would hate to have my foot be raw too. It was a long way down the mountain.

Okay, next person in line for the fun: Larry. It appeared to me that we had to lean at around a forward angle of 60 degrees to not be blown backward. We were into this for about seven minutes when I realized how difficult it was. It reminded me of those old cartoons where the waif, or the old man, or the poor young woman is trudging forward perilously in the snowstorm without the proper protection, slipping, falling, and getting back up again. That was us and it was funnier than a paper cut.

Well, we never found the lake. We found a couple more sink holes, and what we all swore was a lava tube, but nobody fell into that; we just stared down into the darkness and wondered if there were any bones way down at the bottom.

By the time we got back to the edge of the plateau and scurried over, my calves were killing me. Leaning backward at a 60-degree angle is not just impossible, it will wear the heels off of your shoes.

It was getting to be mid-afternoon, and we needed a break. We laid down on the rocks. Believe me, it felt comfortable.

"Well, guys, we did it, and we didn't do it. Are we 'All for One and One for All'?" I asked.

We all made a thumbs-up and said, "Fuck it!"

Remember, we had to walk down this bitch before dark. This knife-edge passage was a challenge in our state (not Hawaii) of mind and physical prowess.

"Let's go, muddas," I yelled.

We all yelled, "*Y E S S!*"

## CHASING THE DREAM

Down the Devil's backbone we trekked, slid, and cussed, until we reached the lush jungle edges of Wailuku again. We touched off our Maglites since it was getting hard to see, and they led the way to our Chariot of the Gods parked in the lot. We did this the best that we could have. Hey, we were alive, bravo!

Back to the story. Believe me, all is related.

"Okay, Kenneth, I will do it." I was living with a woman and her son at this time, and because the work had to be executed in the dark of night, I could do it. The children would all be asleep, and my partner would be in the house with the three kids.

We would brave the West Maui Mountains from the north and prosper. We needed to make a plan, get our seeds started and our shit together. "I am on it!" I exclaimed.

Kenneth actually had plants ready to be transferred, so that cut about thirty days off of our schedule. Great. Since we had two plants to a grow bag, we still had fifteen bags to carry up the mountain and distribute. That is two full trips. The third trip would be water to sustain them for two days. We planned it, and we did it. Everything worked. We went every three days to water and nourish the plants, and they grew and grew beautifully.

The only detail that I was suspect of was our parking place when we did our thing. It was out of the way and hidden, but I was leery. When the plants were ready to harvest, I am talking six feet tall with a shitload of flowers, we made our move.

Our next trip in two days was to cut and run. We had it all together, everything planned out. We parked, grabbed our bags and tools, and set off up the mountain, about a half-hour walk.

When we reached our first baby, it was cut and stripped. The second, third and fourth…all the same. We had been ripped off. By who? The next thing I heard was a few hissing sounds pass by in the trees and crack of rifle fire immediately. I jumped on Kenneth and brought him to the ground. I was guessing it was an M-16 by the volley that followed. Now I was getting the picture. Locals, Vietnam vets—we'd heard the stories—easy, easy money. The West Maui Mountain side was their territory. We fucked up.

There had to be at least two of them, because when one rifle ran dry another started up. They were fully automatic and probably smuggled back to Hawaii after the vets were mustered out, since Hawaii was the R&R for our soldiers.

Leaves and tree branch debris were flying everywhere, but the only thing I could think of was escape. How to? Their muzzles were melting down by now, so we waited for a lull. When it came, I whispered, "Let's move!" We ran up and to our left, through the jungle to the east of them. We hunkered down, quiet. I heard their loud talking where we had been. They were confused and making noise. We moved farther to the east and circled around them. There were more shots directed to the other areas where our plants had been, but we were going away and down, away from them. We could hear them yelling and shooting at nothing.

We reached a dense area of jungle close to where our car was. We lay down and waited, peering through the trees and plants. There did not seem to be a sentry, or any cars, or any danger. I could still hear noise up in the jungle with an occasional shot. Maybe they'd decided to hunt feral pigs.

They got our product, but we had our lives. We ran to the car, unlocked the doors. I slid in, turned the key, and nothing. I knew what they had probably done. I lifted the hood, and sure enough the negative cable was off. I knocked it back on with my fist, shut the hood, slid in—still no shots—turned the key: Voila! I slammed it into drive and peeled the hell out of there.

## CHASING THE DREAM

A few days after the incident, I was thinking about the time and money I'd lost with this endeavor (yes, I was slipping deeper into the dirt), and decided that there had to be a better way to skin this cat. Not knowing why anyone would want to skin a cat, I decided to try an idea that had been kicking around in my brain for a month or so.

I was living in a way-out-there area, not having to worry about nosy people, and decided to do an experiment. I planted a few very outstanding seeds, waited for them to sprout, replanted them, fertilized them, and waited for them to mature. When I saw the first indications of budding, I cut the budding branches, dipped them in a rooting enhancer, replanted them, and waited. With all due diligence, they quickly became quasi-cloned children. The mom stalk was gone, and they were individuals.

I had ten of them in individual grow bags, and I continued feeding them as I had fed their mother plant. This experiment was going really well, because from the air they looked like scraggly houseplants.

There was a guy who every grower feared. He was in charge of "Green Harvest" and was responsible for finding and destroying all their esoteric plants and arresting the growers. I don't believe the arresting thing was all that important to him unless he trapped growers in their patches. Solomon Lee flew around in a chopper, searching out patches in the jungle, sugar cane fields, and private properties. I had no worries; number one, I was right out in the open, soaking up all the sun available with a bunch of scraggly houseplants.

Cutting to the chase, all did go very well. The plants continued to look like ornamental plants, because I snipped off all the new branch growth, leaving only the original branch leaves and the flowering buds. Since they were already forming on the mother plant, when cut they continued growing undisturbed. I only saved one or two buds on each plant, discarding the rest, so all the nutrients were consumed by them alone.

Well, they matured and grew and grew and grew, like none I had ever seen. They just got longer and fatter and longer and fatter, until at harvest each bud was six to eight inches long and an inch and a half in diameter. I felt good in my illicit life, and my product was the talk of the town all the way to Honolulu. I prospered for a while, traveling to Oahu on the local airlines with my product (I even saw Jimmy Buffet and the Eagles one time in 1979; what a concert, hippies and sailors, and it was a mess afterwards) until the trip that ended all trips.

It was slated as a normal business trip, meeting with professional clients, having some family fun, roller-skating in downtown, visiting friends on the North Shore, eating at the Chart House restaurant, and all the regular things that we always did.

We packed all the suitcases to check, drove to the Maui Airport, checked in, and flew to Honolulu. We taxied to the home in Manoa, had a beer, opened my suitcase, and all the product was gone. A chill ran up my back. I wanted to scream, NO! It was the only thing missing; not my $500 camera, not the jewelry, nothing else. Only what could not be claimed as stolen.

We only stayed until the next day, changing our tickets and flying back to Maui, with me looking over my shoulder and expecting the other shoe to drop at any moment. It never did, but when we entered our house on Maui, I uprooted and burned all the plants, and everything in the house that I had used for the business was discarded. That was it for me! (It was a real gas while it lasted, though.) Not too long after this we all left Maui and settled in Florida and Nevada.

All of this was before the "Zombie Diaries" days (where my first book started), but it was so radical that I view it as a diversion from the path. I had to fight my way out. I did, and I survived. Shit, man, I am here today. Some people don't believe that I am, though… humph! One good friend living in Hawaii was at a party a while back, and a few of

## CHASING THE DREAM

my friends were talking about my book *Dream of a Lifetime: Ten Years in the Upper Amazon*.

Another acquaintance blurted, "I thought he was dead."

My friend said, "Well, I believe he could have been many times over, but he's escaped, and even published a book about his escapades."

The acquaintance then exclaimed, "Well, I'll be!" and walked off.

PART 16
# THE END OF DAYS
*Iquitos, Peru, and Jupiter, Florida*
*8-12-2001 to 9-11-2001*

# TWENTY-EIGHT

**THE BABY ONSLAUGHT HAD HIT** August 12, 2001, and we were settling in, starting to feel comfortable with the little one added to our household. Her nursery, which I constructed, was great and worked perfectly for all of her needs. We were getting ready for our trip to the U.S., showing Stacy Ann off and visiting with my mom, sister, niece, and her offspring. My niece had just had a daughter the year before, so there would be "baby energy" in the house.

My mom by this time was feeling the advancement of her age, ailment—COPD—and frailty. It was a good time to be visiting with family. Tickets were purchased for September 10 and we were ready to blast off for Miami on Aero Continente, a Peruvian airline.

We had to fly from our home in Iquitos to Lima, change planes, and continue on to Miami. It was a long trip—twelve hours—for us and a little one with colic. One thing that helped was that Juan Carlos, a Peruvian singer, was on the plane with his family. Carmen and Nayla loved that... very cool!

We traversed the airport in Miami, rented a "shit-box" car and baby seat (first time for that), and took off north to Jupiter.

## NORMAN WALTERS

It is always a good thing to connect with family, but with two new baby girls in the mix we were on cloud nine. Mom was great, like always, with everyone stepping over her oxygen tubes; my sister Tanya and niece Jenny—both in the medical profession—had taken vacation time so we could spend the days and evenings together. Everything looked up and like it was going to be a great time for food, drink, and fun.

After a crazy evening playing with the babies, making margaritas, and laughing our arses off, we turned in knowing we had to get up and take Nayla to the airport in the morning, September 11, to visit relatives in the Philadelphia area.

We arose from our sleep, made a great American breakfast of scrambled eggs with cheese, bacon, hash browns, sourdough toast with orange marmalade, and coffee (of course). Tanya always had the TV running, probably for background noise, and Matt, on NBC, was giving his opinion of the new president or something related again.

Carmen, Nayla, Stacy Ann, and I piled into the rent-a-car, securing little Stacy into her seat and buckling up. I was just pulling the lever into drive when I saw Tanya throw open the front door of the house and, with a panicked look on her face, run toward us with her arms waving in the air.

For some reason I looked at my watch and engraved the time on my brain cells: 8:53 a.m.

I stopped what I was doing and turned off the car, thinking something had happened to Mom or someone inside the house.

Tanya was exclaiming, "A plane crashed into the Twin Towers in New York. A jet, right into the tower!"

We unbuckled, grabbed Stacy, and ran into the house. They had switched stations, looking for more info, and now were on ABC. Live video was running of the gaping hole billowing smoke in the side of the tower, and crying people were being interviewed. We all just sat there, mouths open in shock as they ran the live video. Fire began appearing from one of the holes, and there was complete confusion and shock on everyone's faces.

I sat there, thinking of all the people on those floors and the rescue efforts involved. I saw a new jet plane appear on the right side of the screen and wondered, "What the hell is that plane do..." and at that moment it crashed into the second tower with a giant fireball and black billowing smoke exploding from the hole. Our eyes were glued to the TV screen; I could see cognition sparking in everyone. It was very clear what was happening now. It had to be a terrorist attack of dynamic proportions, nothing anyone could have ever imagined, on American soil!

I felt tears running down my cheeks and looked over at my mom, who was in total shock, and everyone was realizing the same impossible scenario as myself. Tears began to fall all around our house and the entire country...possibly the world.

By about 09:30 a.m. we were all cried out and talked out. I got up to crack open a beer, and Tanya asked, "What is falling from the top windows?"

We all looked closer, and to our horror the debris falling looked like human bodies. My God, people were jumping from eighty-plus stories high to not be consumed by the fires. There were so many onlookers in the streets and rescue workers that there still seemed to be a chance of rescuing many of the people working in the lower offices.

At this time Nayla was going to have a hard time making her flight to Philly, leaving at 10:30 a.m. I called Continental Airlines and asked if the flight was still slated to leave. The receptionist said that she had no information at this time and to call back in fifteen minutes.

It had been more than an hour and a half since the first strike, and it seemed like we could leave it up to the police, firefighters, and various rescue workers. The worst was over. The death toll would be high, but the fires could be extinguished and people would be rescued.

Then the first tower collapsed, rolling over and over itself all the way to the ground, covering onlookers and rescue workers with toxic dust and debris. Total mayhem it was.

I called the airlines again and there was no answer. I called again ten minutes later, and this time there was a recorded message stating that all flights had been canceled.

A few minutes later, the second tower collapsed.

We continued watching like zombies. What else could we do? We all know what happened after that: The heroes on Flight 93, the fourth jet plane crashing into the Pentagon, the grounding of all air travel, all planes out of the air and on the ground, and the final stab, the Seven World Trade Center collapsing to the ground in the late afternoon, due to fires and damage from the collapse of the North Tower.

The cleanup, the search for the terrorist masterminds, the deaths, the injured, the super-heroic efforts of all the rescue workers, everyone's prayers and sorrows, rebuilding hopes and dreams, and overcoming our fears, were all a part of the years to come.

PART 17
# THE STRUGGLE FOR RECOVERY
*Iquitos, Peru, and back to the USA
2003-2012*

# TWENTY-NINE

**THE 9/11 DISASTER HAPPENED** thirty days after our daughter Stacy Ann was born in Peru, experiencing life and death before she had lived for even a second. As I mentioned earlier, we were settling into a new life, and I had just built our dream house in the 'burbs of Iquitos. We were visiting family in Jupiter, Florida, and looking forward to a great vacation, a break from Yacumama Lodge, basically recharging my batteries so when we returned to the grind I would be ready to go.

Unfortunately our projected future did not work the way it was planned. I guess the old adage "The best-laid plans of mice and men often go awry" was being rubbed in my face again. Just when I thought it was safe to go in the water, the sharks appeared.

I believe that is the best way to explain the next course of events on my plate upon arriving back home in Iquitos. First, I learned from the news that many U.S. and international travelers were canceling their flights—to reschedule much later or not at all. There was a large wave of fear drowning most travelers. It really didn't hit me until the calls started coming in from Eco Expeditions, our

Miami booking agency. A cancellation here, a cancellation there, until I realized that "the little pigs were going *wee-wee-wee*, all the way home." All of them.

I called to see if any were re-booking for a later date, and guess what? The answer was… Not yet!

This information was distressing to say the least, but Lawrence and I did still have this sprawling business with a booking agency in Miami, an office in Iquitos, and a tourist lodge far away in the jungle. This probably would have stymied most people, and by November 2001 we decided we were belly-up, but we weren't going to lose the company. We were going to muster out all but a few employees and place the corporation "on ice" with the governmental tax agency, SUNAT, the Department of Labor, Social Security and medical insurance, and AFP retirement. It was our only hope for the future.

Believe it or don't, these negotiations and money liquidations for thirty-five employees took us almost six months to find and pay out. There were no tourists at our lodge or any of the others, and Iquitos was dead. Restaurants and hotels were empty. There were only a few backpackers walking around, and they were desperate individuals.

You might say that we really were on the cutting edge and riding the curl of ecotourism for six great years. One of the "best of the best" and the harbingers of a new profile for tourism. Unfortunately, the break caused by 9/11 also turned the tides, and the next real wave of tourism appeared to be "Fun in the Sun."

But…there is always a positive note if you dig deep enough. There were so many ends to tie up in Iquitos and nothing to do at the lodge that I was able to spend much more time with our newborn baby girl and family. I was not absent all week, returning for the weekends—normal life for us—and we enjoyed more together time. We even celebrated Christmas 2001 in our new home.

## CHASING THE DREAM

Through all of the shutting-down process, there was always the nagging hope sitting in the back bleachers of my mind: "Tourists will start booking again, have faith."

It wasn't to be. Eco Expeditions closed in Miami, and I eventually had to grapple my hopes and dreams to the ground with the realization that I could never support my family in Iquitos without a functioning tourist lodge. The stark reality was that I could only try to start a new type of business. That would take money, and that commodity was in short supply.

I could sell potatoes on the corner—naw, try to start a farm at the lodge and sell my crops at the local market—naw, work for another tourist business—naw, out of the question. Turn tricks? Now that was an idea, but no, Iquitos was too small for that. I'd have to wear a disguise. Nothing that I could think of would bring enough money to support the family.

After battling with this problem for weeks, I finally decided that I would have to start selling our things and prepare to move the family to the U.S. I know, pretty radical, eh? After ten years that would be a mountain of work also, but what else was I doing? Worrying? Fretting? Giving myself hives? The answer was not flapping in the wind, it was having a plan, and so I doubled down, creating a timeline of events.

It was early June when I began my onslaught, and Iquitos, Peru, would have its first "garage sale." I advertised it for weeks ahead of time, with signs affixed on my exterior house wall, stating what I had to sell—yes, the house was included—on the slated date. The list was so long (this was our life), I had to affix another piece of plywood to the other side of the front door to handle all the items.

There were knocks on our door all day long, every day, with people wanting our stuff. If they had the money I sold it right then, and if they didn't I told them to come to the sale. Carmen's friends bought most of our personal items, like the whole nursery, the whole living room setup, kitchen, dining room, bedrooms—it all went.

I had already sold our three tourist boats and motors, using the money to keep the lodge and the few workers left there paid and eating. I kept one very small speedboat and a covered dock (balsa) in Iquitos for my transportation to and from the lodge. These were the last things to go.

By the end of August I had to prepare for the inevitable, our new life in the U.S. Not only would it take money, which I did not have, but time and effort beforehand, finding work and a place to live. I was lucky that Lawrence had some friends in the Miami area who could use my services. I was able to pick up where I'd left off ten years before, doing the same thing. Unfortunately, it was the same pay that I had made back then also. Florida had always been one of the lowest wage payers in the country. But…beggars cannot be choosers.

The next few months were two weeks in the U.S. and two weeks in Peru (for me) to establish my business and find housing. I was successful with both prospects, and we were nestled into our new house in the U.S. for the Christmas season.

I had successfully started a lucrative construction and remodeling business and bought a house and a van with no proof of employment, address, or bank account. This was in the time of the "construction glut" in Florida, 2002, and I had an 826 credit rating. I had actually done all of this on my name and credit rating alone. Someone or something "upstairs" had pulled a few strings for me, and that is why I believe that even though it was a "long row to hoe," good won out… over evil.

It took quite a while—years, actually—to stabilize, but we did. Carmen and Nayla were strangers in a strange new land, with different customs and foods to deal with (it is a good thing they had a cursory

## CHASING THE DREAM

course, living with me at Yacumama Lodge and vacationing in the U.S.). Stacy was cool because she was only one year and four months old when we landed on U.S. soil for good…or bad.

# THIRTY

**IN EARLY 2005,** all the dust had settled and we built up a new head of steam. Lawrence and I talked and decided that if we were able to upgrade and remodel, making it better, we could—maybe—start booking again and reopen Yacumama Lodge.

With these years of idle hands we'd had, I tore down bungalow after bungalow due to so much upkeep, and we were down to sixteen bungalows, from our original twenty-seven. We decided to upgrade at least six of the closest ones with full bathrooms, solar lighting, varnish floors, and more antiquities on display. It was a great plan.

Lawrence had found funding, so this really was a reality. We were going to do it. There still were people wanting to live the rainforest experience, and I started the promotion again to all my contacts, including the information number on our website.

Our project was pretty much complete by late summer 2005. Lawrence then got deathly ill in Peru on his last finishing trip, and it basically grounded him. I kept putting out the word and responded to inquiries. And by early 2007, I began getting actual bookings again.

My old buddy Steve "the white water man" brought the christening group, January 2008. Plenty of people, plenty of fun, and everything unfolded okay.

*Steve and group on the "Lazy River?"*

Now it was late February, and things were looking up. I had confirmed and had money deposited for groups in March, April, June, July, and a tentative one in September. I was thinking that by the end of the year we could be floating again if this kept up.

Uh oh! Watch out for those tentative thoughts!

The call came in the morning, March 8, 2008.

I answered the phone, "Hello."

It was Gloria. "Hola, Norman?"

"*Si, buenos dias.*"

"No, Norman, *hubo un incendio en el albergue a noche.*" (No, Norman, there was a fire in the lodge last night.)

I sat there speechless for a bit then asked, "How bad? Was anyone hurt?"

"Alfredo had to be taken to the hospital in Nauta for burns on his arms and feet. He broke down the flaming fire breaks that you constructed in the walkways to prevent fires from spreading in the roofs of the walkways. They worked perfectly; it stopped the spread of the fire, but the falling embers burnt him," she told me, holding back the tears, I could tell. She continued, "But there was severe damage. The main building, the kitchen, the dishwashing area including the solar batteries and inverter, and the employees' dining room are all gone. Every artifact, decoration, and book are gone!"

I sat quiet for a few seconds, and then asked, "Will you send pictures as soon as possible?"

"I am on my way now, calling from Nauta. As soon as I return to Iquitos I will send them."

My next job was to call Lawrence and alert him to the situation. I was thinking, though, that I'd had about enough of this shit, and wanted the road to straighten out. My tires were wearing down. Our deal had always been that I would run the place day-to-day, and he would make sure that the money was there, like always. Sure, I had to augment the money once in a while, but that was business.

Well, this was a whole new ballgame. We are talking a lot of bucks to rebuild. Should we say "Fuck it!" or keep the faith and keep on truckin'…that was the question. Lawrence was devastated, of course, and wanted to see pics. I said I would send them to him as soon as I got them, and we left it at that. Look at the pics, and then talk again.

## CHASING THE DREAM

After seeing the devastation, we both just wanted to cry. This was our baby: conceived, built, run, maintained, and enjoyed...what more can I say?

After a day or two more we talked again and decided to clean it up. We had five employees living at the lodge, two of whom were in the hospital, one with burns and the other with appendicitis. As soon as they could work again, the crew would put all its combined effort into dismantling and cleaning up the area so nothing of these destroyed buildings existed. No reminders. Unfortunately I had to return all the money to the clients and cancel their tours.

This was March of 2008. It took me almost two and a half years to rebuild the lost buildings, smaller this time but looking the same. While I was at it I decided to demo six more bungalows and leave ten. We were talking self-preservation here. The less we had, the less work and employees we had to maintain. There were no greenbacks coming in...just going out.

This worked pretty well, and all the wood from dismantling everything went to the rebuilding. Sure, some of the boards have burn holes in them, but who's looking? Then we could at least have the medical groups and the water engineers staying at the lodge again. That would give us a little compensation and help pay the bills.

All of a sudden we had this great idea. We could get a permit to cut some of the trees on our land, open the business again as an import/export supplier, and ship the sawn boards to the U.S. to sell on the open market. Great idea. Lawrence had been kicking this around with Craig, a friend of ours, and we entered into a three-partner project that should have made us some money. All we needed was a portable sawmill, a team of men, the permits, and my ability to open the company back up again, which I did.

I went to Peru in late 2009 to start the process in motion. It took me two trips and a bunch of waiting to get the permit, but we still couldn't get the saw sent to Peru, past customs, and in my possession, so I decided to buy some of the local wood for the first shipment, send it, and call that our first hit. It was good, and it sold. We went for a second round, and that worked out also, but we still weren't cutting on our property. We were just buying it directly from the sawmill, shipping it out as an exporter, bringing it into the U.S. as an importer, and trucking it to the shop.

Eventually, the Lucas portable sawmill was in Iquitos, and I had to go there to spring it from customs. Of course I needed an agent to represent me, and they gave me a bunch of shit about the replacement parts, but I did get it out, and I planned the next trip to Peru for cutting wood on our property with legal permits. I was so delusional, it was a wonder I wasn't foaming at the mouth.

I'm telling you now: All my life I have been ready for anything because I knew I could pull it off, and I did. This next project—cutting

## CHASING THE DREAM

down 150-foot trees and milling them into lumber in the middle of the jungle with a crew of twelve men—was really pushing the envelope. No machines to destroy the jungle, just a chainsaw, brute force, the portable sawmill, and log jacks.

Once cut and the tree was down, we had to cut it into thirteen-foot sections, roll one section out of line, assemble the sawmill around it, square it off, and begin to cut it into boards, back and forth, back and forth, back and forth, ad nauseam.

*A good four-section tree*

*Brute strength, 1,500 pounds*
*Yours truly cuttin' 'em up*

All the cut boards had to be hand-carried out to the boat, approximately fifteen to twenty minutes. While I was cutting, they were carrying. Each tree had three to four sections—thirty-six in all—and I cut for two solid weeks. We ended up with 5,000 board feet of lumber, or 500 boards, more or less. That's a lot.

I was in the jungle for three weeks that trip, and by the time I finished my penance, completed the itemized inventory, and stacked all the boards to dry, I was raggedy with a budding beard.

*My motley crew, the end of the road, 2012*

## CHASING THE DREAM

I swore to myself and to my two partners that my cutting was over and I would never cut another tree on the property…period. Sell the Lucas mill. I didn't care! I never wanted to see it again. Of course I had to see it again because I had to find a buyer in Peru and sell it, and I did!

I ended up trading the sawmill for wood. Nobody wanted to buy it, and it sat around for a year. I finally found a broker with a possible need for the mill. He had cumaru and blood wood sitting in his warehouse that he couldn't get rid of either, because they were beams with very large dimensions.

We made the swap: the saw and all its extra parts for 5,000 board feet of hardwoods (valued at $12,000 in Peru and $50,000 in the U.S.). We just had to bundle it up and ship it out. We still had a valid permit for exportation, but it took about thirty days to get all the inspections and documents in line. We packed it up on pallets, rented a truck and forklift, loaded it up, and off it went to the dock. Yee haw! We were halfway to heaven.

Weren't we surprised when the dock supervisor came out to the truck and told us that his computer showed that our company was shut down, so he couldn't accept the cargo? Then he laughed and told us that it didn't matter anyway, because there weren't any ships anymore. The Peruvian shipping line had been shut down because of illicit activities. I guess they were moving drugs. No more ships, no more wood shipments.

To make a short story long and bring the cows home, I'll wrap this damned tale up. That wood sat in a rented warehouse for five years, having to be moved every year to clean under and fumigate. When Iquitos flooded it had to be raised and put on blocks. I am talking a royal pain in the arse.

I put out the word that I would accept offers. So when my sister-in-law found a buyer and the offer was acceptable, I took it. We had already lost so much money on this deal that the pittance we received didn't even begin to plug the hole.

When the saw disappeared I said, "YAY," and now that the wood has disappeared I say, "Double YAY." Casey Kasem said, "The hits just keep on coming," and I'm not even keeping score anymore…one foot in front of the other. That's me!

## PART 18
# THE CARBON PROJECT
*Yacumama Lodge*
*2012-2018*

# THIRTY-ONE

**IN 2012, WHEN I TOLD** Lawrence that I was not cutting any more trees on the land that we had been protecting for twenty years, he sort of chuckled and asked, "Would you like to know what I have been researching for the last couple of weeks?"

Still fuming, I responded, "Sure, let me in on the stupid joke."

Well, he began spinning one of his webs that he is so good at. "Have you heard anything about carbon offset projects?"

"I guess it is a bit funny that you should mention that after I said what I said. Yesterday I listened to a dissertation on NPR about carbon emissions, carbon footprint, carbon offsetting, and how it relates to the rainforests" (as I was bumper to bumper on 826 trying to shut out the exhaust fumes).

He laughed and began telling me about a program that could eventually end up paying us for protecting the land in Peru. The people he had talked to at Virginia Tech made it seem like it would be a slam-dunk because of our unique situation (sounds good).

He was starting the paperwork and following up with documents, with titles for land tracts. He said that I would need to accompany technicians to the lodge two or three times to do their biological and technical work. Then there would be another man coming to check their work. Then it would all go through quickly.

Have you ever heard of the term "confidence men"? They have that name for a reason. They have a nickname too… "con men!" I truly believe that the head guy had a bag of carrots in his pocket and ran Lawrence through a bunch of hoops on his own negligence and inattention to detail.

I went to Yacumama Lodge with the VT boys three times. Yacumama's 500 acres weren't included in the carbon project because it was not private land and was a part of corporate holdings. The two parcels of Lawrence Bishop and Lawrence and Adriana Bishop, about 7,500 acres, were the backbone of the program, and he controlled it.

They had to find GPS locations, tag trees and their surrounding biomass. I think they had twenty-six GPS locations and tagged twenty-three. They worked hard and diligently, but everything was paid for, and a lot of money was changing hands. No loss for them.

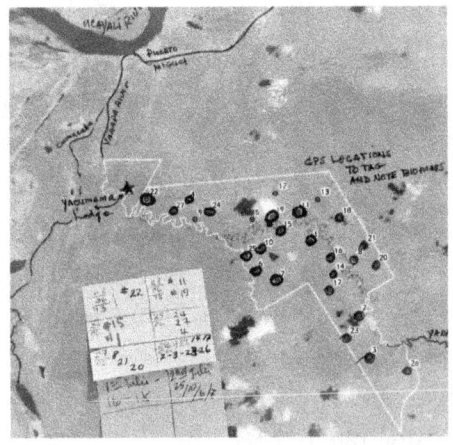

*GPS pinpoints for assaying*

## CHASING THE DREAM

All that I remember them saying is, "Your project will move very quickly because you only have one *owner* of the land, not villages and indigenous tribes involved. It should be only a year or so before you see the credits."

The above map is of the depicted properties. The top triangular tract is Yacumama property, our shared parcel. The large outlined piece (with the black GPS pinpoints) is actually two tracts of land belonging to Lawrence Bishop and Lawrence and Adriana Bishop, the carbon project.

I referred to this in Chapter Two. The two parcels were purchased in 1993, and I supervised and signed the documents, titles, and the registrations for Lawrence and the Dolphin Lady. I over saw the repurchase of the DL's 3,250 acres (when Lawrence repurchased it from her) and protected these parcels from depredation for twenty-six years, bringing the protection services of the flora and fauna—INENA—to arrest the thieves and return our fallen trees five times, to donate to the village. It was a bitch and a half. The thieves hated me for protecting the jungle and threatened me many times.

So, as you can see, I had a vested interest in the carbon project, to say the least. Yacumama Lodge, my only holdings in Peru, was closed. That meant no dividends or incoming money. I was very surprised when the paperwork arrived for my percentage of the dividends from the carbon project.

This project had cost Lawrence a lot of money, and it had cost me *countless* hours (in twenty-six years), yet it still wasn't complete and running, with dividends yearly. There were still questions to be answered—they said—and Lawrence could not keep up with the ordeal due to a physical illness. Everything went on hold. It was a disastrous hit for all the investors involved.

The "great expectations" and promises from the VT guys were

forgotten, and more work had to be done, according to the auditors. Guess what? More money too! It is still unsettled as of December 21, 2019, but Lawrence is working on the details again and who is to say?

PART 19

# WE MUST SELL THE LODGE IT IS THE ONLY WAY OUT

*2018-2019*

# THIRTY-TWO

**COMING AROUND** to April of 2018, Lawrence asked me if I could pay half of the monthly nut for the lodge (we'd always had the agreement that he would pay the nut and I would run the day-to-day and solve the legal problems, unless there was a real problem, and then I would help monetarily). I was trying to cut my expenses, work less, and enjoy life a bit before the Grim Reaper came to visit. I was living my seventieth year and wanted a break.

I responded, "Okay, but I am going to put out my feelers to sell the lodge." We batted around prices and came up with $750,000. This was an operational tourist lodge in good repair, which included 500 acres of jungle land, "In Title!" Such a deal.

Well, nobody bit, and we came down and down in price until we were at $200,000. Sill, nobody wanted to invest. I was not going to go down any farther. We'd just keep on keeping on, for a while!

We were entering September, and still no bites. The best offer I had was from the director of an NGO wanting it for free, but that disappeared when they decided they couldn't keep up the monthly nut.

This was getting ridiculous. There was an investment of more than $1.75 million, and we couldn't even give it away to a good cause. Was that the "wet kiss at the end of the hot fist" or what? The end of the dream was when a *friend* asked me to transfer it to her name, and she would run it and keep it going. That was the moment that I decided that I would resurrect Yacumama Lodge or close it down, give all wood and construction materials to the village of Puerto Miguel, and just hold on to the 500 acres. Fuck everybody!

Then the next kick in the balls came: My partner, my bubba, told me that he was out of it because of his health problems, and Yacumama Lodge was all up to me, to keep going or let it go. At this point I said, "Okay," and took on the whole monthly nut myself. By the way, the monthly nut was money for three people, food and all expenses for the two at the lodge, all repairs and maintenance, plus anything unusual that happened 2,600 miles away from me.

Bear with me just a little while longer. We are coming up on the end of the story. I promise and I pray!

I invested more money into the infrastructure, trying to upgrade it, thinking that I would be able to contact my old clients and start again. I hosted one more medical group in February of 2019. I constructed a new thirty-by-thirty-foot dock, serviced all the mechanics, repaired all the bungalows and roofs, and had a great last hurrah! Thirty-seven passengers and no complaints. Thank you, Great Spirit!

I awoke from the elation of actually pulling off a group of that size, everything working, and terminating a project from hell with no money made. Time trudged on, and I survived March and April. In May of 2019 I tried to resurrect groups from the old clients for August. I almost succeeded, there was interest, but everything was moving too fast for the old farts, and both groups fell apart. At that point, I decided to book my flight to Iquitos, Peru, shoot the poor old horse (Yacumama Lodge)—you know—put her out of her misery. Give my helpers a

## CHASING THE DREAM

bunch of money for their time served, donate all the wood and building articles to the village, and walk away a new man. Yee haw!

• • •

Not so fast...about a week and a half before my departure date, I got a communication on Whatsapp: a guy wanting to talk about the sale of the lodge. Okay...that's what I'm talking about. His company wants to resurrect and save tourism on the Yarapa River. He wants to repair and upgrade a lot of Yacumama's facilities, build another tower, inundate the internet with advertising, and construct a waterfall and natural pool. He is a very industrious young man who knows what success is all about because he is a success. He has a new website and is booking passengers as I speak.

I did pay my Peruvian friends a good sum of money for the years they stuck it out with me, and they will better their lives with it. The Great Spirit care for them all.

So I guess you could say I held out until the eleventh hour and accepted the path I would have to take. Fortunately, I may not have to drag my cross down the rugged road of pain and sorrow, but I will not hold my breath. I will just breathe easier for a while. When June 30, 2020, arrives, I may then walk out a new man. I guess we will see, won't we?

Thank you for listening, I have removed a great weight from my shoulders, hopefully not putting it on yours.

I am still alive!

We will see what the future brings. Remember, this is a continuing adventure, LO-fricking-L!

# EPILOGUE

**YOU KNOW,** I have always believed that things like life's struggles and joys, death, good situations, bad situations, and anything we tend to dwell on, weave their way through our lives to create, put finishing touches on, or terminate the pattern of our lives. We all try to find meaning and answers for our happenings, but is it possible that sometimes these occurrences are true serendipity? This is a question I ask myself frequently.

All the building blocks necessary for this "Dream" adventure that I have written about were necessary for me to truly experience the color, texture, and depth of this experience. But I also believe that there are always a few boomerangs mixed into the brew to keep us on our toes. I have been smacked in the back of the head a few times.

We were actually one of the forerunners of the eco-touristic travel movement in 1992. We lived through the height of the boom and rode the wave until the destruction of the Twin Towers in lower Manhattan on 9-11-2001.

After everyone woke up from the shock and began traveling again, ecotourism began its trek to extinction. The new surge of travelers—from the USA—were looking for fun and diversion. Cruise ship guest lists grew exponentially, as well as Vegas and Caribbean Island getaways. We tried to resurrect ecotourism, but the interest was so low that I believe this particular brand of tourist went into a state of deep sleep, like—*Wake me up when people care again.*

I do believe that there is a possible opening in the collective human mentality and our desire to exist. This force—being exhibited by the "Young People" of our world today—could give birth to a new trend: awareness, altruism, and respect for our Mother Earth. "Every living thing!" A new form of ecotourism could emerge, focusing on seeing and appreciating what we have left.

Welcome, all ye believers!

# ACKNOWLEDGMENTS

**FIRST AND FOREMOST**, I would like to thank and recognize Emily Hitchcock, editor, director, and all around professional friend. Thank you for all of the negotiating telephone conversations we've had getting these "Dream" books out, and a fist bump to the art department at Columbus Publishing Lab.

# ABOUT THE AUTHOR

**NORMAN WALTERS** is an artist, writer, and adventurer currently living in Florida. He has played music in NYC, worked at Woodstock, and lived in three quarters of the world, including three major rainforests (India, Hawaii, and the Peruvian Amazon).

His first book, *Dream of a Lifetime,* depicted the first two years of his adventures in Peru (1992–1994) building an altruistic tourist eco-lodge in the middle of the Amazon jungle (110 miles from civilization).

*Chasing the Dream* is a continuation of this adventure that spans the next fifteen years (1994–2019) in the Peruvian labyrinth of business, love, negotiation, deceit, thievery, oppression, ethnic interaction, and beauty.

Norman spends his time creating and restoring fine art pieces, writing songs (and now books), searching for The Life of Riley, and spending time with his family.

The author encourages you to contact him with questions about the book. Connect with him on Facebook @NormanWalters, or email him directly at newaltersdesigns@gmail.com. Artwork, including many pieces inspired by his time in Peru, can be found here: normanwalters.com.

For more information about Yacumama Lodge, Google "Norman Walters, Yacumama Lodge."

If you enjoyed *Chasing the Dream*, discover more of Norman's unique brand of adventure in *Dream of a Lifetime*, his first book.

**Available at Amazon and Barnes & Noble,
or ask for it at your favorite bookstore.**

www.ingramcontent.com/pod-product-compliance
Lightning Source LLC
LaVergne TN
LVHW041609070426
835507LV00008B/175